The Art of Herbs: Growing Herbs for Beginners

by Greer Jackson

Acknowledgments

To Grandad, whose watermelon patch next to the garage is still the inspiration for all my gardens.

About the Author

G reer Jackson is also the author of Foraging for Wild Edible Plants: The Natural Food Lover's Guide to Identify and Cook the Abundant Free Food Around You Right Now. He is also an avid gardener. In 1988, he grew the largest zucchini in the state of Michigan. In 2012, he grew 20 pounds of sweet potatoes in a single container. Today, he focuses more on flavor than size or quantity, except he still finds lettuce leaf basil a wonder. His favorite herbs are French tarragon, green shiso, and celery leaf. He has grown fruit, vegetables, and herbs in temperate regions, Mediterranean climates, and even deserts.

Write to Greer and share your inspirations, ideas, and questions about herbs. He reads every message that comes through at greer-jacksonbooks@gmail.com.

Table of Contents

Get these free printables to help you design your masterpiece.

Looking for more herb inspiration?
Try out these 50, totally free.

My garden is my most beautiful masterpiece.
–Claude Monet

Chapter 1

Purpose– The whats and whys of herbs

M ary Thompson's garden, on Tillman Street, was Versailles wrapped in chain link. In my memory, there was never any wind back there, only breezes, the kind so soft they could only pick up smells, nothing else.

There was one of every kind of rose you could want to smell, rows and rows of them, and one of every kind of fruit a kid would want to eat. In fact, it was in this yard that I snuck my first grape, fresh off the vine, a milestone for any city kid.

As I think about it now, that garden was probably super useful. When you have dozens of great grandkids running around, a bush full of berries and a tree full of pears is not a luxury.

But that yard must also have been a place of rest for my great-grandmother, Mary, too. I've never seen anyone as serene as when she stood dead smack in the middle of her garden, under her arbor.

And for some reason, I remember her standing there often, in a gray dress or a blue one. Sometimes the flowers were in bloom. Other times there were just leaves. But anyone that saw her face in those moments would want to grow things.

And so, I garden too.

I wouldn't describe any of my gardens as Versailles quite yet, but I'm getting there. I'm probably most proud of Snoopy Garden. I called it that because if you turned your head and squinted just right, you'd see that this garden was shaped like a Snoopy head.

In case you're wondering, the answer is no. No; I didn't plan on putting a big Snoopy head in the middle of my yard. Like a lot of things in gardening, it just happened, and so I went with it.

I ended up putting fruit trees and garden beds all around Snoopy. And in the middle, right on Snoop's eye, I put a bench. Sometimes I would sit out there, on that bench, and watch the pomegranates and horseradish grow.

And sometimes, I'd whisper to the baby kumquats to see if that would keep them from falling off the tree while still pea-sized and green. It didn't work. It's funny though, because the autumn I moved out of that house, the kumquat tree exploded with fruit!

I've never been sure what to make of that tree. Yes, I know kumquat trees take a few years to bear fruit. But I've always wondered if maybe, just maybe, tree wanted me to stay and thought its display would persuade me. Fruit trees can be show-offs like that.

But don't worry. Most herbs won't play these kinds of win-lose games with you. With leafy plants, what you see is what you get. And I like that about them.

On the other side of town from Snoopy Garden is Circle Garden. There are no benches here. This is not a place to sit. This is a walking garden.

A walk around Circle Garden is a little ceremony that only a few people experience. And I'm honored that I'm one of those people.

Here's how you walk in Circle Garden. Every two steps or so, you stop and pick an herb leaf, and you smell it. Then you rub the leaf between your palms and smell it again. And all throughout the walk, Candace is your guide. She cares for the garden and runs the women's shelter that uses it.

Every time a new client arrives at the shelter, Candace does this garden walk with them. She said this helps the women to relax into their new life situation, which is usually better than their last.

None of the plants in Circle Garden are unique. They are varieties you could find in any bloated big-box store. But still, this little garden walk, of less than ten minutes, is very restful.

Sure, part of the reason a Circle Garden walk works is that Candace is a skilled professional. She curated the herbs, their placement, and their layout. But it's worth mentioning that she chose herbs, not vegetables, not decorative plants. Tending to herbs is so restful that it can even comfort people during one of the most challenging parts of their lives.

Of course, Candace helps her clients with the functional, like shelter and clothes. But she also needs to support them emotionally. And her herb garden is a part of that support. Circle Garden serves a clear purpose in her community of care and support.

So, Candace has a compelling purpose for growing her herbs. So do I. And so did my great-grandmother. This brings me to you. What's your purpose for having an herb garden?

Maybe that's an abstract question. But I think it's important to start here, by thinking about your purpose. Whether you can name it yet, or not, that purpose is why you're reading this book.

Your purpose is why you will put your fingers in the dirt. It is why you will prune, and weed, and harvest. Purpose is what will make your garden a reality.

Whatever your purpose is, this book is here to help you get that purpose out, onto paper, and into the ground, growing....

Ok, then. Let's get started.

What's an herb?

Most people say herbs are the fragrant leaves we use to add flavor to food. They are not the chief ingredient. They are an accent. But they offer so many additional flavors to food: spicy, bitter, astringent, numbing, sour, savory, sweetish, or even chili heat.

Sometimes, people include a few seeds and flowers as herbs. Mainly, I'll be referring to flavorful leaves as herbs in this book. But I'll also include a few flowers and seeds here and there that are super interesting.

Herbs have been a part of human life for thousands of years. Of course, we have used them to flavor our food. But they are also a kind of medicine. And we use them in ceremonies.

My focus in this book will be the culinary uses of herbs. Maybe I'll write another book about these other uses. All three are important, but there just isn't room here.

I should also mention that this book isn't about spices, the accent flavorings made from the root, stem, seed, fruit, or bark of plants. Spices tend to be dried and have more potent flavors than the delicate leaves of herbs.

Spices and herbs have this in common, though. They are both flavor enhancers. You just use them differently. But this book is about gardening and the fresh stuff you can pull from your plot or planter.

Now, let's get some terms out of the way. Maybe you've heard the term "herbaceous plant." In this context, herbaceous refers to plants with soft, greenish stems. On the other end of the spectrum are woody plants. These plants have brittle stems with bark on the outside.

Culinary herbs include plants with both woody and herbaceous stems. Oregano, rosemary, lavender, and others all develop woody stems, but they are still herbs. Mint, parsley, and dill are all herbaceous, with green stems.

Using the word "herbaceous" in a book about herbs is confusing. So, I'll refer to the groups as delicate herbs and woody herbs or tender and woody. And this book will cover both categories.

What's in this book?

You deserve an herb garden that suits you, where you can have fun or maybe enjoy your place of peace. Getting you to that goal requires a focused book with specific information to help you design and implement the herb garden of your dreams. So, here's what will be covered here.

This book will:

1. Show you how to create a garden of manageable size with a manageable amount of maintenance for your lifestyle.

2. It will help you make a list of the things you get excited about eating. And it will help you figure out how to get those plants growing.

3. It will help you design and plant a garden that looks and smells good, whatever that means to you.

4. It will help you design a garden that can develop as your knowledge of herbs develops. One of the things I like most about herb gardening is that there are always new thrills to keep me engaged. Your garden will do the same for you.

5. It will tell you the tools you need to make it happen.

6. It will give you plenty of inspiration and information about using and storing all these beautiful herbs.

If that sounds good to you, chapter two will serve you well. It's a compact summary of the steps you'll need to take to grow your garden. After going through it, you'll see how easy this can really be.

Chapter 2:

Tasks for growing your herb garden

You can get a doctorate in the topics discussed in this book. But I don't think that's your goal. You want a garden that's more pleasure than work, more inspirational than soulless. That's where this chapter comes in.

Suppose you know the essential parts of your herb gardening project. In that case, you can focus on them and the inspiration they bring rather than the more boring bits. That's what this summary of the steps to starting an herb garden is designed to do for you. It's a bird's eye view to prevent you from getting overwhelmed, from getting in the weeds. Instead, you can focus on what will give you results and joy.

The tasks: Herb gardening in a nutshell

I didn't plan it this way. It just happened–really–that the steps to herb gardening break down quite nicely into ten steps.

Whenever you feel overwhelmed, just look at this page to see what you need to do next.

1. This book is about fragrant and tasty plants that will take your food from ordinary to extraordinary. Start by making a list of herbs that fit that bill for you. Your list should include

the things you love, the plants you can't live without. Also, put a few plants on the list that seem unique to you. Maybe you don't know much about them right now, but you want to learn. Next, put a few herbs on the list that are common in the cuisines you most like to eat. Finally, add some representing flavors you enjoy: spicy, bitter, sour, sweet, refreshing, etc. What flavors do you gravitate to? Don't worry about how many plants are on the list right now. Just put everything down that you think about.

2. Next, get to know your climate and terrain. You need to know when the best times to plant are in your area. Obviously, planting dates will vary depending on where you live. Some places have an all-year growing season. Others have three short growing seasons. If you live in a cold place, the date when the ground freezes really matters. If you live in a very hot place, how much summer sun your plants get is crucial. Figure out what factors are important in your area. But this doesn't need to change what you want to plant. It just affects when, how, and where you plant.

3. Step three is to figure out which plants on your list do best when the weather is cooler and which thrive when the weather is hot. You want to know the necessary steps to make growing a plant possible. For example, if your area doesn't allow you to grow a plant outside when you want, you still have options. Consider a greenhouse or shading, some indoor pots, or pots that can be moved inside when needed.

4. Now, find areas in your space where you can grow these plants. Most people think of a garden as a discrete or consecutive space. But that doesn't have to be true. Put your plants where they will thrive and look beautiful. Maybe you use several parts of your outdoor space. Maybe there are herb

plants in each room of your house. It's all about placing them where it makes sense for your situation. Any area where you can water them and access them is fair game.

5. Next, it's time to source the plants. Determine which plants on your list are best grown from seed and which are best as cuttings or seedlings. You can buy seeds and seedlings from your local garden center or online. And don't forget about farmers' markets. Don't buy anything yet. You're just sourcing things now. Buying comes later.

6. Now is the time to edit your list and make your garden design. Maybe you don't have enough space for everything you want. Or maybe it's the opposite. You don't have enough plants to fill up your space. Or perhaps you have some climate constraints. This is the time to decide whether to nix plants that won't do well in your existing conditions or whether you want to create spaces with those conditions. You're the boss.

7. Now that your list is completed, step seven is to prep your plots or pots. This means getting any tools you need. This may also mean adding nutrients to the soil. Or, maybe you will use prepped potting soil. No matter what, make sure your soil is well drained and loose so that air flows through it. You may also want to mark out your plots, so you know what's growing where. This may mean sticks, rope fences, or those cute little signs with the names of the plant written on them.

8. This is the fun part: planting. Plant outside for the part of the year you're in. If it's cool, plant the cool-season plants. If it's warm, grow plants that like those temperatures. If you want to grow plants outside their comfort zone, this is the time to modify some plots. Add shade or cold protection as needed. If you're planting indoors, just make sure you can control the

conditions to keep the plant happy or put it in a place that most suits it. But generally, you can plant indoors at any time of year. You did it. You made a garden.

9. Plan on watering your garden at least once a week. Of course, if it's rainy, you can water less. Also, plan on weeding at least once per week. You don't need to pull every weed. Just get the ones that are encroaching. Also, use mulch to keep new weeds down to save yourself time in the future.

10. Replace plants throughout the season as needed. When something dies or runs its course, put something else in its place. Do the same when the weather changes. Replace plants on the down cycle with ones that will thrive in these changed conditions.

Sometimes things seem complicated because we don't know where to begin. Once we get started, everything flows. That's how herb gardening is, too. Just put these ten tasks on repeat, and you'll have an Instagram-worthy garden all year round.

Recipes Part I: Sides, Soups, and Salads

Getting to Mmm

I put cinnamon in the eggs. I was twelve, maybe thirteen. It doesn't matter. I was big enough to pick up a full-sized cast-iron skillet and hold it over flames without killing myself.

And on this day, I thought, why not get a little crazy? Why not pull open that spice cabinet and see what's going on? A full spice rack is and has always been like the best cross between a potion bag and a toolbox for me, utterly irresistible.

My grandmother Josie once told me she could always tell when I visited her house because her spice rack would be all jumbled up. It's no wonder, then, that I'm writing a book about herbs.

It seems that I've always been interested in exciting flavors. But I didn't know what the heck I was doing when I was little. For example, those eggs I mentioned earlier, they were horrible, trauma on a plate. There was no mmm there. But hey, you've got to start somewhere, and this is my flavor origin story.

Thirty years later, I'm still playing around with flavor. I'm still working on my mmm. In fact, just this last Wednesday, I was at it again for my friend, Raul, instead of for family.

I made a warm fava bean salad. It had spearmint, parmesan, lemon zest, a poached egg, and bacon lardons. In other words, this dish was firing on all cylinders: zesty, umami, refreshing, and creamy. It was all there.

I served my creation with buttered biscuits and homemade apple sherry garnished with rosemary and lemon zest.

My 2021 sherry is a bit like a slightly sweet, oxidized vermouth. And that's how I use it. It's nutty, acidic, and with a base note of apples so of the fall that it'll have you pulling out your cable knit sweaters!

My sherry makes a delightful apple spritz with just a bit of sparkling wine added to it. Think of an Aperol spritz, just with apple flavor. Or it's great just over ice and with garnishes. That's how we enjoyed it on this Wednesday.

But, the immediate star of this menu for Raul was the biscuits. I could tell that he loved them right away. They were fluffy and just at the cravable edge of saltiness, no more. These biscuits were deserving of two bites right out of the gate. And, they were deserving of an mmm, my first from Raul that day. I was pleased.

The salad was his next victim. As Raul dug in, I could feel my face moving into that wide-eyed, expectant look, waiting for his verdict. But, I caught myself and focused on my personal mmms for a few seconds.

For me, even though there was spearmint in the salad, it was a bit salty too. Two salty things… together. No mmm. Raul concurred.

Next, I saw Raul pick up his sherry with the rosemary sprig. And finally, "mmm," along with a head wag. He'd found it, the right combination. The key this day was the sherry.

Raul didn't say this, but I think his mmm was elicited by the classic and balanced salty/sour combo we all know and love. That same combination is the reason people love salt and vinegar potato chips. It's why people buy those giant dill pickles you see in checkout lanes everywhere. It's the reason people put lime juice and salt in beer.

The version of this classic combo Raul enjoyed, though, was enhanced by the refreshing zing of herbs. If you hadn't guessed, the herbs on this menu — rosemary and spearmint — came from pots on my patio.

I love that my herb-filled menu that Wednesday was about the journey to mmm. This was not an immediate hamburger mmm: fat, salt, done. It was a quest.

For me, getting to mmm is better when it's like a game, just with flavor and your tongue instead of a joystick and a screen. You're going to encounter a few unexpected turns along the way. And you'll have to try several maneuvers before the mmm reveals itself. But that's part of the fun.

Herbs can be an exciting addition to your mmm quests if used correctly, from sprouting the seeds to tending the plants to experimenting with them in your food. Each step in growing your herbs is part of the journey.

Some dishes are easier to experiment with than others on your way to deliciousness. If you want some low-stress but exciting mmm journeys, I suggest starting with the dishes in Recipes Parts I and II.

Sides, soups, salads, and bevs are less complicated to make than most main dishes. They're low-stakes since you aren't playing with an expensive protein in most cases. And they can really show off the best of an herb's flavors.

Start riffing on the recipes in these two sections to get your feet wet. Build on the balance of flavors already in the recipe, but switch out my ingredients with your favorites. Make them your own. Then, test them out on friends and family for some mmm-quests of your own.

Twenty-one-leaf salad with champagne vinaigrette

Because it's all herbs, you'll get a flavor bomb in each bite of this salad. Of course, you can change the name if you don't have 21 kinds of herbs in your garden. A seven-leaf salad sounds good too.

Pick a mix of greens with different flavors: refreshing like mint, bitter like parsley, sour like shiso, sweet like stevia, and earthy like oregano. Getting a good balance of flavors will make the salad tastier.

Also, you're probably not going to use real champagne for this recipe. A grocery store sparkling wine will do. No one will ever know. You can still call it champagne vinaigrette.

Making champagne vinegar from any sparkling wine is an option too. Just age it for a month. Put a piece of plastic wrap over the top of your container and poke a few holes in it. It's a great way to make sure that half-used bottle of sparkling wine doesn't go to waste. Or just mix some sparkling wine in with the dressing, as this recipe suggests....

Here are a few notes to help make this recipe a success:

1. The method below to mix your dressing into your salad prevents the herbs from getting crushed. It's a super simple thing to do. And the results do seem better to me.

2. Many of the recipes in this book will say 'salt to taste.' Here's what that means. I once heard a TV chef say that we know intuitively how many times we need to shake the salt shaker over our food. That's how we start with finding our taste. Put as much as feels right, then actually taste and adjust until the flavor is what you want.

3. Normally, salad dressings should be a bit salty because your salad greens don't have any salt on them. Taste the salad after it's dressed to be sure that the salt level is where you want it. Add a few shakes more at the end, if needed, and mix them in.

Ingredients:
6 cups herbs, chopped
1/2 tbsp sparkling wine
2 tbsp olive oil
1/2 tbsp lemon juice
1 clove garlic sliced into big pieces (optional)
Salt and pepper to taste

1. To serve four people, you'll need a total of six cups of greens. About 1.5 cups per person is a good amount. So, that's ⅓ cup of each kind of green if you're using 21 in total. Pick and wash ⅓ of each cup of the kind of green you need.

2. Dry all of your greens very well so that the dressing sticks to them.

3. Pick one leaf or kind of herb as your base. Because I always have lots of oregano, that's what I start with. Then cut or tear every other herb to the same size or smaller than your base herb.

4. Mix all the prepared greens together in a bowl twice as large as you need.

5. This salad is great on its own. But you can add additional textural elements such as edible flowers, creamy cheeses, and crumbled crackers. You might even add orange slices that are cut down to size.

6. Mix the sparkling wine, olive, vinegar, garlic, salt, and pepper together.

7. Pour the dressing onto the sides of the bowl above the herbs.

8. Push the herbs up into the dressing until fully coated.

9. Serve the salad on chilled plates and add any garnish you like, such as cheese, edible flowers, or crunchy things.

Tabouleh

Normally, this Middle Eastern salad is made with parsley, mint, and green onions. But spring onions will be just as good in this. And you can add any other herbs you like. I think oregano and marjoram would be great in this salad too.

Most recipes call for curly parsley. But you can get away with flat leaf if that's all you have. If you don't have bulgur, you can use couscous or even rice. I sometimes also add cucumber, feta cheese, and toasted pita chips to this recipe.

Ingredients:
¼ cup extra virgin olive oil
2 tablespoons lemon juice
⅛ cup bulgur wheat, cooked
1 ½ cups parsley
1 medium tomato
1 green onion, both the green and white parts
⅛ cup fresh mint leaves
⅛ cup oregano
Salt and pepper to taste

1. Cook the bulgur until tender.
2. Season the bulgur with salt and pepper.
3. Mix in the lemon juice and oil olive into the bulgur and set aside.
4. Wash, dry, and chop the vegetables.
5. Remove any excess water from the tomatoes and other vegetables.
6. Stir chopped vegetables into the seasoned bulgur.
7. Served on a chilled plate.

Herby mashed cauliflower

If there's someone in your house that doesn't like cauliflower, try this dish on them. It's soothing, like mashed potatoes. Plus, it's buttery, creamy, and herby. It's a combination no one can resist.

You can use fresh or frozen cauliflower in this recipe. But frozen is a bit easier. It's already chopped and cooked. So, it saves you a few steps. Using frozen puts this dish in the realm of a weeknight quickie. But fresh obviously has more flavor.

Try different herbs in this dish. Dill, rosemary, marjoram, mint, tarragon, and thyme would also be delicious here. If you don't have goat cheese on hand, use yogurt or cream cheese instead.

Ingredients:
1 head of cauliflower
2 tbsp butter
2 oz goat's cheese
1 clove garlic
¼ cup fennel leaf
¼ cup carrot leaf
¼ cup dill fronds
Salt and pepper to taste

1. Chop the cauliflower into florets.
2. Boil the florets in salted water for about 15 minutes until tender.
3. Puree everything in a food processor in batches.

Herb soup with rice

This warming soup is comforting and hearty. It makes a great starter at any time of year.

You want your leaves to be just wilted for this recipe. If they are still somewhat fresh, you'll get more herby flavor from them.

Sage leaf crumbles would be delicious with this dish. You could also add a bit of cheese. And feel free to substitute the leaves I put in this recipe with a mix of your choosing.

Ingredients:
4 ounces breakfast sausage
3 large cloves garlic, minced
1 1/2 teaspoons fennel seeds
1/2 cup beer
2 quarts low sodium chicken broth
3/4 cup cooked rice
15-ounce can of butter beans
6 cups baby arugula leaves, roughly chopped
2 cups parsley, chopped
1/2 cup celery leaf, chopped
Salt and pepper to taste

1. In a soup pot, cook the sausage through and break it into small chunks like chili meat.

2. Add the garlic and fennel seeds and cook until soft and fragrant.

3. Add the beer and broth to the pot and bring to a boil for about 5 minutes.

4. Lower the heat to a simmer and add the beans and rice to the soup. Cook until warmed through.

5. Season the soup with salt and pepper.

6. Remove the pot from the heat and add your leaves.

7. Serve in warmed bowls.

Chapter 3:

Tools to grow herbs

All you really need to start your garden is a bit of soil, a seed, and a stick. You can even just buy an herb gardening kit from your local big box store. It just depends on your needs and your level of motivation and experience. But these tools will make the work of planting and maintaining your garden easier. These tools may be the difference between an overgrown mess and a bountiful, beautiful, fragrant garden.

You may have some of these already. Pick and choose the ones you need and want from the list below.

In and outdoors

Snips/kitchen scissors: These are great for harvesting leaves. Sometimes, the delicate leaves rip if you pull them by hand. And torn edges tend to rot more quickly. The kitchen scissors make sure you have a clean cut, which prolongs the life of your harvest. It also makes it easier for your plant to recover. The sturdiest pair of these can cut through bone. You may not need a heavy-duty pair like that, but it's your choice.

Pick a pair with stainless steel blades so they don't rust. No matter how hard you try, your shears will get wet. You should also get a pair that fits well in your hand, depending on whether you're left–or right–handed.

Kitchen scissors are great for food prep too. Sometimes, scissors are easier to use than a knife. That's especially true if you need to make anything more than a straight cut.

Outdoors

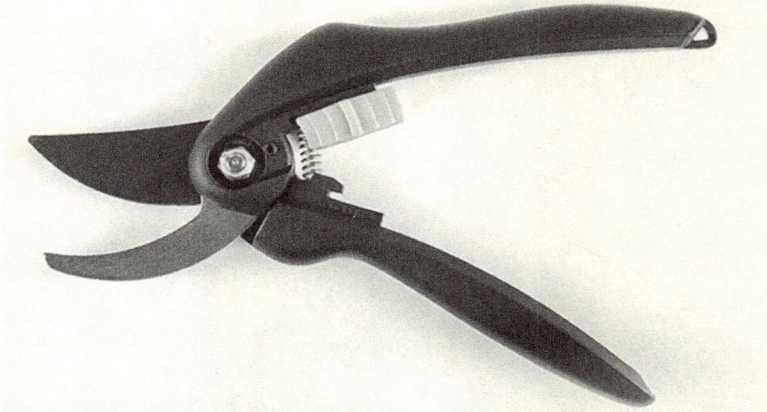

Pruners: These are a more heavy-duty version of snips. They will help you take out woodier stems and branches. This can be a dangerous and painful task unless you have the right tool. So, pick up a set of these.

Much of the same reasoning holds true for pruners as for snips. They make a cleaner cut, which does less damage to the plant. And they will for sure get wet a time or two. So, stainless steel blade is the best material for pruner blades.

You'll need a soft covering over the handles. Pick a pair that feels good in your hand when you press them close, and you're set.

Pruners and snips are not interchangeable. Because of their shape, pruners may not even cut a leaf. And snips are nowhere near sturdy enough to deal with a branch.

Watering can: You can use a hose with a sprayer to water your plants, but be careful. The water pressure can damage young or delicate plants. A watering can lets out just enough water to hydrate the soil around your plants without damaging them.

Some watering cans have removable heads that allow you to water in a single stream or several streams. This kind of flexibility is a pleasant bonus to have.

You'll probably see a number of models in galvanized steel. Avoid these. They will corrode over time. Paint will provide some protection. But, if the paint is scratched, you lose that protection. And it's hard not to scratch something that is around a lot of sticks and twigs.

You can find watering cans that are over a gallon or smaller ones that are just about a pint. Pick one that's appropriately sized for your job. I find watering my plants to be one of the most relaxing tasks in the garden when I use a watering can. Yes, this is the fun part!

Gardening gloves: Of course, gloves will protect your hands and nails from thorns or anything else you don't want to touch. They will also help keep them clean. But if you get a pair with a grip, they will also help you get a good grip on slippery things.

Look for a pair that is sturdy but still light. Leather works well. So does mesh with vinyl over the fingers. It just depends on your style and budget.

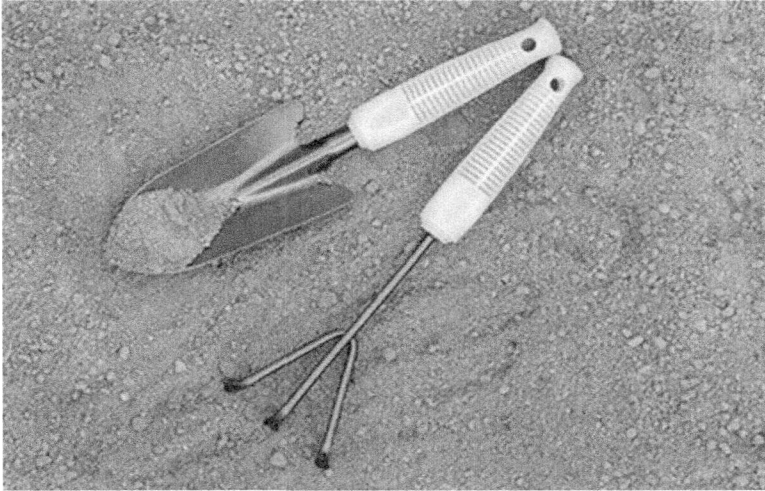

Hand shovel: Use this tool for digging holes, uprooting plants, loosening the soil for planting, for adding soil to pots, or even marking rows and boundaries. It's a very versatile tool.

Most of the models you'll see will be made of aluminum. This is a good choice. First, it's lightweight. It's also water resistant. It will corrode but is a pretty durable material. The Aluminum Association says that over 75% of the aluminum ever made is still in use. So, it should last a good while for you.

Indoors

Seed starting kit: These are kits you can buy online with all the necessary components. They are also available in many garden centers and home improvement stores. Typically, they have a black plastic base with cups where you put your dirt and your seeds. The base is covered by a clear dome to keep in moisture. You can buy these kits with four cups all the way up to 60 seed cups.

I've used these kits many times and will again. Their biggest benefit is that the dome keeps in the humidity while allowing light in. Their biggest drawback is that, depending on the model, getting the seedling's dirt plug out of the base can be challenging without crushing it. Then, the kit isn't reusable anymore.

You can also use soil plugs. It requires a small machine, but they aren't tough to make. You just wet some soil until it clumps together. Then, you mash that soil into a block. Most soil block makers make blocks with a small indentation in the top for the seed. Once you add your seed, just cover it up with a bit of dirt if that kind of seed needs it.

The benefit of soil blocks is that they are ready to go into the ground or the pot as soon as the seedling has a few true leaves. The drawback is that you still need a base for your soil blocks to water them without everything getting wet. A dome to hold in humidity is also a good idea. But, once you have your base, dome, and soil block machine, you can use all of them year after year.

Some people germinate their seeds in a wet paper towel first and then add them to the soil blocks. But it's usually not necessary. No need to do extra work. Starting with soil blocks should work just fine.

Leaf spinner: This helps dry your herbs before you use them. Wet herbs don't hold dressing or sauces well. So, cooking with dry herbs is best.

This tool is composed of a sieve that sits in another container on a spine that allows the sieve to turn. The top has a handle that you push or turn to make the sieve spin. Spinning throws the water off the herb leaves and into the other container. This is a must-have if you cook or use herbs in large batches.

Outdoors

Soil Knife: This is one of the more optional tools. But there are certainly times when it comes in handy. This includes any time you need to cut something thicker than string, such as root balls and heavy-duty twist ties. But you can also use them for weeding, transplanting, and digging holes.

Most models will have at least one serrated edge, which is great for sawing through vines. They also usually have a ruler on the blade. This is great for planting seeds or bulbs that do best when sown at a specific depth.

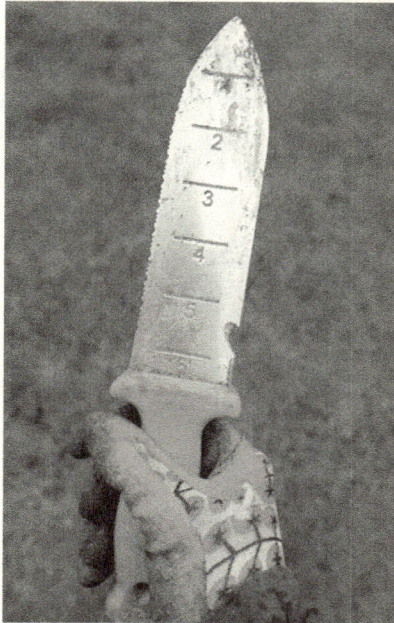

Hoe: This is an ancient tool. It's what people used to sow all their seeds before the plow was invented. There is evidence of its use in ancient Egypt and Sumeria or southern Iraq.

This tool can do much of what your hand shovel can do, just without the need to bend over. Use it to loosen soil, chop weeds or dig holes. If the hoe you choose has three tines on one end, you can use this side to spread or remove mulch, compost, or leaves.

Garden Shovel: Use your shovel to move dirt, dig holes, make trenches, and more. It does heavier-duty versions of what your hand shovel does. So, you'll need it if you have a larger garden. It also keeps you from bending down to do all of this. Think of your shovel as a major labor-saver.

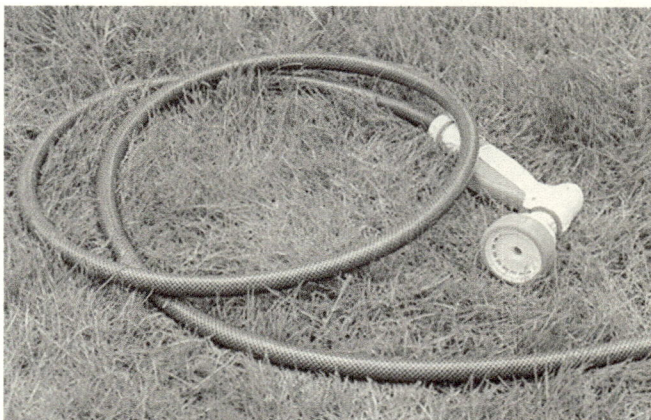

Hose: Like your shovel, your hose is a labor saver. It gets the water close to plants without lugging a bucket around. Even if you use your watering can at the end, your hose still saves you the labor of getting water over to where it's needed.

A light-duty hose will work in small gardens. But, they are the least durable of the lot. They kink easily and are easily cut. If any of those things are concerns for you, consider a hefty model. But I have 250 plants and can get away with a light-duty hose.

Garden shoes or boots: Wet feet are never fun. Accidentally getting your shoes and socks wet while watering is always possible. If it's cooler out, you have another reason to wear garden shoes. Because cold and wet feet are never fun either.

Then there's the mud. Having shoes you don't mind getting muddy in and can remove when you come into the house will make gardening much less work for you.

Sometimes, it's the little things that add up and that create overwhelm. The added sweeping and mopping from getting mud in the house is something you want to avoid.

For storage

Ice Cube Tray: You may be wondering what ice has to do with herb gardening. It's a storage method. You can save pesto, chimichurri, and other herbal sauces in the trays.

You can pretty much store any herb in oil in these trays, too. This is a great storage method if you have extra herbs around that you don't want to go bad. We'll talk more about storage in chapter 9. So, don't worry.

Herb Keepers: These are specialized containers for storing herbs in the fridge. They help keep them fresh without you having to concoct a storage method. They are large enough to hold a bunch of herbs. The stems sit in water to help keep the bunch fresh.

For extremes

Shade covers: Use this if you live in a sunny place or just want to plant some delicate plants. The mesh comes in different opacity levels depending on how much light you want to get to the plants.

Frost covers: These are similar to shade coverings, except the fabric is literally a blanket that helps keep in warm air rising from the ground. Think of these as mini-greenhouses. Use one of these if you want to get plants in the ground really early in the year or if you want to keep them in the ground really late into the growing season.

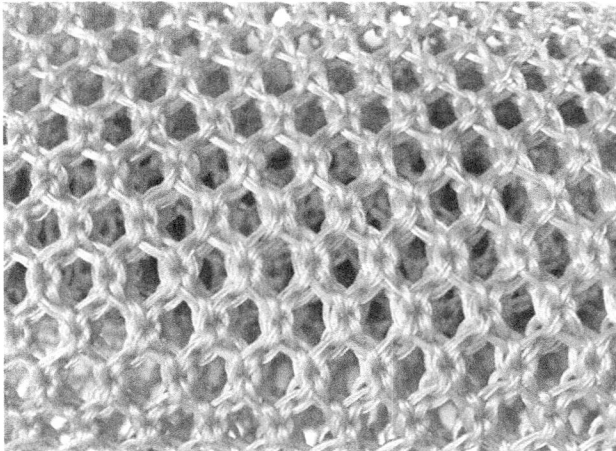

Wind netting: This netting does precisely what you think it does. It reduces wind in your garden and the damage it can do to plants. It also keeps the stuff the wind blows out of your garden: dust, weed seed, and debris.

The best of these nets can reduce wind by up to 75%. But if you don't want to buy a specialized net for this, you can use sunshade netting hanging up on poles like a fence.

If you don't want to buy all these items, here's my list of the ones that'll help you the most.

- Kitchen scissors are a must, in my opinion. They will greatly improve the quality and extend the life of your herb harvest.

- Get a hand shovel. You'll use it every time you're in the garden for something.

- Get a watering can that is appropriately sized for your garden.

- The other important thing, in my opinion, is a seed starting kit. If you're an intermediate gardener, buy a good seed starting kit. It's the beginning of your herb-growing journey. If the first few parts don't go well, you won't be set up for a good outcome.

If you're a beginner, I don't recommend starting from seed. Buy healthy-looking seedlings in a store where you can chat with knowledgeable staff.

And if no seedlings are available, get an herb-growing kit. An herb-growing kit is similar to a seed starting kit, but also comes with the seeds and instructions to grow them. It's pretty foolproof.

You can buy many other things to help your gardening: knee pads, brushes, seats, stools, and even weeding robots. The point of this is to have fun. So if you're into gadgets, go for it. But if you like a simpler approach, that's fine too. The point here is to get the tools that free you up to do more of the stuff you want and less of the stuff you don't. So, keep that in mind while shopping.

Ok, so you're in a really good place right now. You have an overview of the steps required to make your herb garden dream a reality. You also have the tools you need to make it happen. Next, you need to figure out what you want to plant. That's what's coming up next.

Chapter 4:

Choosing what to plant

I start looking through seed and plant catalogs at the beginning of every year—usually in January. I'm on the list to receive several print catalogs full of herbs. But I also look online and at my favorite brick-and-mortar stores. It's super inspiring to think about the fun stuff I'll plant in just a few months.

I like to try a few new plants in my herb garden every time I plant. I decide what to try by considering the options in these catalogs. Some options I'll keep. Some I'll save for the future. Others may never happen at all. But considering these options is an important step. It's the first concrete action toward making my garden a reality.

I'm doing more than just dreaming by looking at these catalogs. This is how I start my list of the actual seeds and plants I want to buy. And that is my goal for you, a concrete step toward your herb garden project.

So yes, your first step should be making a nice list of plants for your herb garden. Check out my herb garden printables download for a template you can use. The links to it are at the beginning of the book.

This won't just be any list of plants. It will be a list that suits you. It will be a list you can get excited about. It will be a list that motivates you to keep going through the rest of the steps to make your garden a reality. To make this list, include a few herbs from each section in this chapter.

Where else do I look for herb ideas?

In chapter five of this book, there are over 50 herbs listed with information about the cuisines where they are used, flavor combinations, growing information, and more.

Another great resource is *The Flavor Bible*. If you're a cook or interested in food, this really is your bible. Whereas the plant list later in this book is organized by herb name, *The Flavor Bible* includes every ingredient imaginable, not just herbs. So you can look up a fish, for example, and look through a list of herbs and other ingredients that go well with it.

You should also check out print and online catalogs for inspiration. These will list all kinds of herbs, maybe things you've never seen before. That's the fun of it. Catalogs may not have much information about using the plants. But usually, they will say tons about growing them. My favorite online catalog is Baker Creek Heirloom Seeds.

Also, check out your local garden center and farmers' markets. Not only will you be able to buy plants and seeds there. You'll actually be able to talk to experts that know about your local conditions. You can probably use Google to find your local garden center. But farmers' markets might be a bit more of a challenge. You can use the USDA National Farmers Market Directory to find one near you.

What do you like to eat?

Include herbs from your favorite foods in your big list of herbs. What three dishes could you eat daily for the rest of your life? For me, that would be a smoked leg of lamb, fresh naan, and sweet potato pie. So in my herb garden, I'd pick herbs that would add some exciting flavors to those foods.

Rosemary, mint, and thyme are all great with lamb. Parsley, celery leaf, and dill would all be nice sprinkled over freshly buttered naan. And carrot tops, marjoram, and rosemary would all be nice with sweet potatoes. Look at that. I already have a list of eight herbs that I should definitely plant in my garden.

Choosing herbs by cuisine

If someone asked what you wanted for dinner tonight, what would your response be? Chinese? Thai? Indian? Peruvian? Whatever that answer is, it should also tell you something about what should be in your herb garden. You can bring the freshest version of that cuisine into your kitchen whenever you pick the fresh herbs used in those cuisines.

There's a list of herbs by cuisine below. You'll notice that many herbs recur across cuisines. Adding these herbs to your garden will give you a lot of versatility in what you can cook. But add any and all of these to your list if they interest you.

United States
White sage, fennel, echinacea, bee balm, yarrow, mugwort, wild ginger, sassafras

Mexico
Cilantro, Mexican oregano, epazote, papalo, spearmint, avocado leaves

Peru
Cilantro, black mint, chincho, epazote, fennel, lemongrass

Italian
Italian basil, rosemary, parsley, marjoram, oregano, sage

Chinese
Scallion, chives, coriander, curry leaf, lemongrass, Thai basil

France
Parsley, thyme, bay leaf, French tarragon, chervil, chives

Morocco
Saffron, hyssop, marjoram, oregano, sumac, thyme, coriander

India
Curry leaf, saffron, cilantro, fenugreek, turmeric, mustard

Vietnam
Cilantro, culantro, lemongrass, shiso, Thai basil, spearmint

Nigeria
Scent leaf, lemongrass, bay leaf, shallots, chives, uziza

Choosing "rare" herbs for your garden

Maybe there were some herbs you hadn't heard of in the section about cuisines. This is where you can dig in and learn about new flavors.

You can start by adding a few new plants from a cuisine you already like. Or you can step into something entirely new for you. In chapter five, there will almost certainly be herbs you don't know much about. Include some of these in your list just for fun.

Also, think about using different parts of a plant as herbs. For example, radishes, carrots, peppers, peas, beans, celery, garlic, onions, and leeks all have edible leaves. Maybe these are already in your garden. Why not make use of these leaves since you already have them around?

These common vegetable leaves are great sprinkled over and through your dishes. And you kind of know what to expect since you are familiar with other parts of the plant already. For example, pepper leaves are slightly spicy, as you'd expect. Onion tops taste oniony. Radish tops…. You get the picture.

Experimenting with herbs is not as complicated as you might think. Most herbs fall into a flavor category: refreshing, spicy, bitter, sour, sweet, et cetera. Pick an herb you don't know much about, but that falls in a category you like. Let's say you choose sour. The next time you make a recipe that calls for sour sorrel, for example, swap it out for curly dock leaves, which are also sour.

Another way to experiment with herbs is to add a blend of herbs from the same flavor family rather than just one. Let's say that a recipe calls for oregano. Marjoram and oregano have very similar flavors. Try adding both to your Italian seasoning blend or chimichurri. Both of these recipes usually include oregano. Imagine how much more enjoyable they'll be with both.

The whole process of herb gardening is about learning new things and exploring. That's why you should add a few plants from this "experimental" category to your list. They make for great gardening and culinary jaunts.

Choosing herbs for practical reasons

So far, we've looked at your flavor preferences and other things that should get you especially excited about having an herb garden. These should have all helped grow your list. Now, we'll add some parameters that might cull or grow your list.

The first and most practical concern is climate. Where you live, some plants will thrive. Others will just do alright. Still, others will never take hold. You will only be able to plant things that work with your climate. Use PlantMaps.com to help you determine how your climate overlaps with these needs.

The herb descriptions in the next part of this book will provide information about the season each herb needs. Use Plant Maps to help you determine how your climate overlaps with these needs.

There will be plants that love your climate. Maybe you want to plant a ton of those. On the other hand, it may not be worth growing something if you can find good quality options at a reasonable price in your local grocers or farmers' market.

But you just might want to grow a plant that's super expensive, rarely available, of poor quality, or very perishable. It may be worth the effort to try growing this plant, even if your climate isn't perfect for it.

If you absolutely love a plant that isn't naturally suited to your climate, you'll need to think about the best place to put it. Maybe there's a spot inside that will work. Maybe you can add some grow lights to one of your rooms to make it suitable.

I had a coworker that added humidifiers to the room with his plants. Maybe you can even make it work outside with a shade covering, frost covering, or windbreak. Maybe you just have to water a bit more. Or if the ground gets too wet, you can try raised beds with well-aerated soil. Everything is possible depending on how important a particular plant is to you.

The point is not to keep you from growing what you love. The point is to figure out how to make growing these plants possible if that's what you want.

Finalizing your list

Maybe other herb books suggest that you start with the practical matters of picking the herbs you'll grow. But I disagree. What if what grows easily aren't things you like very much or don't excite you? That's a recipe for losing interest in your garden. And we don't want that.

I want you to have a garden that inspires you when you look at it. I want you to have a garden where you see a plethora of tasty dishes just waiting to be made. You should see pots or beds full of treats when you look at your work.

So, start with plants in category one: the things that really inspire you. Add a few plants from cuisines that you love to eat. Pick a few from the experimentation group to keep the novelty level of your garden high. Then, and only then, consider a few practical plants. You want to fill up your beds or pots with things that are exciting for you first.

Now you have your list of plants that you want to grow! How thrilling is that?

Herb Garden List For Year :

THE NAME OF THE HERB YOU WANT TO GROW	WHY YOU WANT TO GROW IT : FAVORITE CUISINE, FAVORITE FLAVOR, EXPERIMENTAL, OR HEARTY	IT'S A COOL-SEASON OR WARM-SEASON HERB	SOURCE	SEEDS OR SEEDLINGS
Shiso	Fave	Warm	Baker Creek	Seeds
French Tarragon	Fave	Cool	E-bay	Seedling
Celery	Fave	Cool	Baker Creek	Seeds
Angelica	Experiment	Cool	Amazon	Seedlings
Chamomile	Experiment	Either	Farmers	Seeds
Chervil	Experiment	Cool	Amazon	Seeds
Thyme	Cuisine	Cool	Big Box	Seeds
Sorrel	Cuisine	Cool	Bakers Creek	Seeds
Sage	Cuisine	Either	Farmers	Seeds
Chives	Hearty	Cool	Big Box	Seeds

Don't worry about the number you have on your list right now. In the later chapters, we'll discuss the most important ways to cut your list if needed. For right now, still focus on fleshing out your list. You can always cut later if needed.

Recipes Part II: Drinks

The great thing about these drink recipes is that once you get the ratios down, you can start experimenting with different herbal flavors. Just swap out the herbs in these recipes with some other fun ones.

And the very first recipe in this section for vermouth is an excellent opportunity to start experimenting. If you don't have the herbs listed in the recipe, find a replacement using the herb flavor chart at the back of this book.

Another fun thing to play with using this recipe is seasonal variations. Maybe the version below is for spring. But you could also do a version for the hottest part of the year when the shiso, basil, mint, and thyme will be in full gear.

In the early fall, you could try a version of this recipe with evergreen herbs that are still available. Rosemary, sage, savory, and lavender would make an excellent base for an autumn cocktail.

Adding the optional sherry will push the flavors in the fall version of this recipe even deeper into the cold season. And because the sherry has spirits in it, you'll be able to keep this bottle long enough to enjoy it during the holiday season. Just cork it well and store it in a cool, dark place.

I also want to suggest, with all humility, that you try this recipe even if you think you don't like vermouth. This recipe is nothing like the bottles you find in your local grocery.

This homemade vermouth recipe is closer to a sangria than to a commercial vermouth. But this aromatized wine relies on herbs instead of the intense fruit flavors from the orange, apples and grapes you get in sangria. It's a much more delicate take on "spiced" wine.

Sweet white vermouth

Ingredients:
1 bottle pinot grigio
1 1/2 cups sherry (optional)
1 1/2 cup honey
1 lemon peel
1/2 tsp nasturtium flowers
1/2 tsp nasturtium leaves
1/2 tsp sorrel leaves
1/2 tsp rose petals
1/2 tsp chamomile flowers
1/2 tsp lemon balm
1/2 tsp gentian root

1. Combine ingredients in a pot and bring to a boil.
2. Immediately remove the pot from the heat and let it stand for five minutes.
3. Cool the mixture in your refrigerator.
4. Once room temperature, add the optional sherry if desired.
5. Store in a sealed bottle and place in a cool, dark place.

Lavender lemonade

Lavender is very strong. So be careful with how much you add to your syrup. If it gets too strong, just add a bit more lemon juice to your mix. This will get your drink back in balance.

Ingredients:
1 tablespoon lavender flowers
4 cups boiling water
1 cup sugar
1 1/2 cups freshly squeezed lemon juice

1. Bring the water to a boil.

2. Dissolve the sugar in the water.

3. Turn off the heat and steep the lavender flowers in the water for 30 minutes.

4. Cool the lavender tea to at least room temperature.

5. Add the lemon juice and adjust to your taste.

6. Serve in a chilled glass with ice.

Lemongrass lemonade

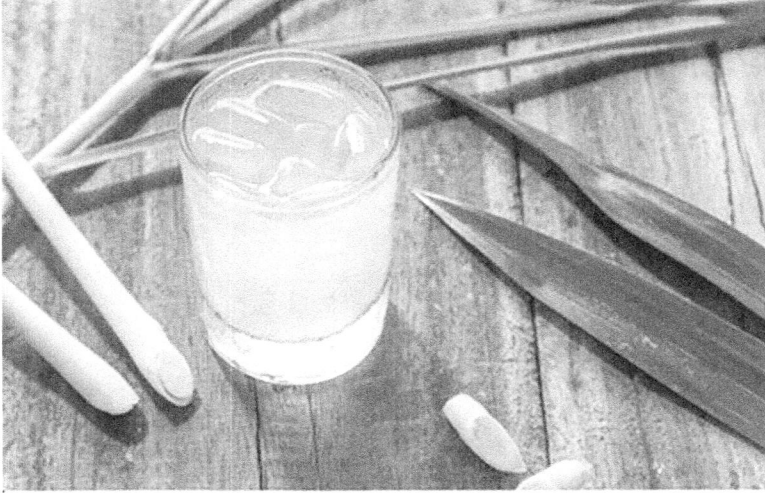

This is a variation on the lemonade above. Just swap out the lavender flowers with a total of one tablespoon of lemongrass to make a lemongrass simple syrup.

Lemongrass martini

Ingredients:
½ oz of lemongrass syrup
2 oz gin or vodka
½ oz dry vermouth

1. Pour ingredients into a chilled glass with ice.

2. Stir until the liquid is chilled.

Bay leaf tea

This is a very centering tea. It's also a superb source of vitamin C.

Ingredients:
2 cups water
2 bay leaves

1. Bring water to a boil.
2. Steep the bay leaves for at least three minutes.

Rose Petal Tea

Ingredients:
2 tbsp of rose petals
2 cups water

1. Bring water to a boil.

2. Steep the petals for at least five minutes or until they lose their color.

Fresh herbs really belong anywhere you put them.
~Alex Guarnaschelli

Chapter 5:

The herbs

What herbs do you have in your spice rack right now? It's probably the more popular herbs, the ones you see mentioned in recipe books most often. You probably use many of these "popular" herbs in your day-to-day cooking.

Swapping fresh for dried is a simple way to add a bit more flair to the dishes you love cooking. That's why this chapter—maybe more than any other in this book—will change how you eat. And that change will definitely be for the better.

Here's a simple substitution for using fresh herbs instead of dried ones. For every teaspoon of dried, add one tablespoon of fresh.

There's a bit of a story about each of the herbs in this chapter. You need a reason to plant these herbs. And that reason can't be just flavor alone.

These little anecdotes will hopefully get you super interested in an herb or two you hadn't thought about before.

There are 53 herbs in this chapter, from plants that become trees to herbs that you can use as garnishes to plants that you probably don't think of as herbs but have around already. Here we go.

Agastache

This herb has been used as a breath freshener and tea. Use this herb in much the same way you use mint.

How to plant: You can grow Agastache from seed or cuttings. Start seeds indoors about one month before your growing season begins. Plant your new seedlings outdoors when they are at least four inches tall. This herb doesn't need great soil. But water it regularly while it's taking root. It also self-seeds easily.

Mature size: Up to five feet tall and one foot wide.

Water: Agastache is relatively drought tolerant. Water it deeply once per week. If the ground doesn't dry out, switch to once every two weeks. Make sure the soil isn't consistently wet.

Sun: Full sun

Cuisines: Chinese

Maintenance: Pinch off top leaves to help it get bushier. Cut back flower stalks before they go to seed. Don't trim after mid-summer.

Warm or Cool: Warm

Flavor: Minty

Annual or perennial: Perennial, but it dies back each year.

Recipes and uses:

- Use with the same fruit you'd combine with mint

- A dessert of peaches, agastache, chantilly, lemon zest

- Make a tea blend with agastache, mint, bee balm, and other refreshing herbs

- Make a simple sugar syrup flavored with Agastache to flavor anything you want

- Freeze this syrup to make ice pops

- Make a salad with barley, bulgar, lentils, and an agastache yogurt dressing

- Other flavors that would pair well with agastache: cucumber, mango, watermelon, feta cheese, basil, lamb, chicken, pork

Angelica

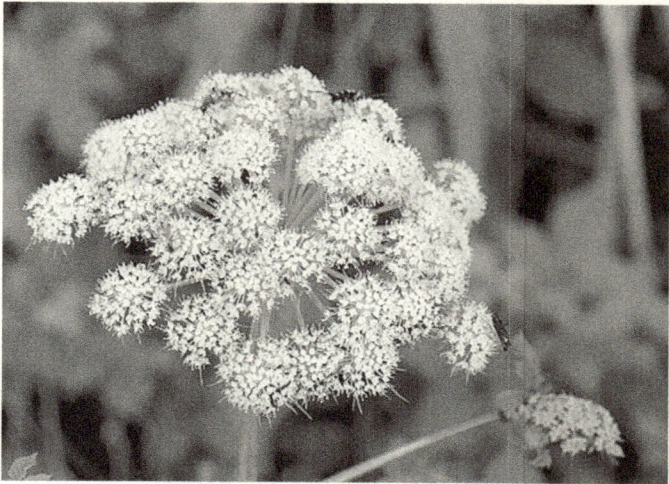

If you like Chartreuse, you'll love the taste of Angelica. Most people extract a fragrant oil from the roots and fruit. But the leaves have a similar flavor and are great to eat.

How to plant: You can plant seedlings that are at least four inches tall.

Mature size: It can grow up to eight feet tall. Only plant one every five feet.

Water: Plant in an area that gets consistent water.

Sun: Full sun

Cuisines: Chinese, French

Maintenance: Angelica doesn't like dry conditions. So, this plant is an excellent candidate for mulch. But it doesn't want its leaves wet either.

Warm or Cool: Cool

Flavor: Licorice

Annual or perennial: Perennial

Recipes and uses:

- Make a tincture, bitters, or infused alcohol
- Make a compound butter with pink peppercorn and orange zest
- Use this compound butter to make butter cookies
- Make a refreshing sorbet with angelica and lemon zest
- Make an angelica and pear compote for toast
- Zest up your chicken soup with angelica, coconut milk cilantro, and lime

- Other flavors that would pair well with angelica: tarragon, goat cheese, seafood, especially mussels and clams, tomatoes, oranges, beets, and root vegetables

Arugula

Most people think of arugula as a lettuce. But it's also an herb. So, let's call it a salad herb. You can also use it in sauces or chop it finely and use it as a garnish.

How to plant: Arugula grows quickly, and its seeds can be sown directly in soil. Plant seeds ¼" deep. They'll germinate in about a week. You can speed this up by soaking them for a few hours before you plant them. It grows well in pots and indoors.

Mature size: Less than one foot tall.

Water: Every other day. Water the plants every morning if you live in a dry, hot place.

Sun: Full sun

Cuisines: Italian, Argentine, Californian

Maintenance: Plant new seeds when you pull mature plants. This way, you'll have a fresh supply all season.

Warm or Cool: Cool

Flavor: Spicy, peppery

Annual or perennial: Annual

Recipes and uses:

- Mix arugula puree into buttery pasta
- Arugula beet and goat cheese salad with pine nuts
- Make arugula pesto
- Top a pizza or flatbread with arugula pesto
- Sautee with goat cheese and mushrooms to fill an omelet
- Mix arugula with couscous, cheese, and cucumbers to make a salad
- Other flavors that would pair well with arugula: salmon, shrimp, steak, grilled foods, tomato, peas, apple, pear, stone fruit

Avocado leaf

Yes, you can eat avocado leaves. They are used as a tea, a flavoring in tamales, and in other steamed dishes. You can toast them if you want a stronger flavor.

How to plant: Plant at least 30 feet from other trees and 10 feet from buildings. The roots need a lot of room. Plant your seedling when it's at least six inches tall. Avoid planting in high-wind areas.

Mature size: Avo trees grow up to 40 feet tall.

Water: Water two times per week during its first year. Once a week is sufficient when the tree is established. Let the tree dry out between waterings.

Sun: Full sun

Cuisines: Mexican

Maintenance: Trim early in the growing season.

Warm or Cool: Warm

Flavor: Anise and licorice

Annual or perennial: Perennial

Recipes and uses:

- Use as a bed for grilling shrimp
- Wrap whitefish with avocado leaves before steaming
- Wrap tamales sweetened with orange in avocado leaves
- Toast your avocado leaves and add them to your favorite pot of beans with onions and a piece of fatty pork
- Sprinkle ground avocado leaves, black pepper, and garlic powder over seared tuna
- Steep toasted leaves to make an earthy and spicy tea
- Other flavors that would pair well with avocado leaf: cumin, coriander, tarragon, caraway, Chinese five-spice, fennel, pineapple

Sweet Basil

Because basil is so popular, there are many varieties out there. There's Thai basil, African blue basil, black basil, lettuce leaf basil, and so many more. But here, we're focused on sweet basil. It's the most common variety you'll find to grow.

Sweet basil is versatile enough to cover the Italian classics: pesto, Caprese salad, and Margherita pizza. But the flavor will also work in most other dishes that call for basil: omelets, noodles, sauces, and more. The one exception is Asian food. Thai basil is a better bet there.

Sweet basil leaves are a glossy green and grow up to four inches long. They are oval-shaped and end at a point. The leaves curve downward and have wavy segments between the veins on the leaves. The fresher the leaf, the wavier it will look.

How to plant: Basil is great in containers. It can be grown from seeds or seedlings. If planting from seed, do not sow deeper than ¼". Once your sprouts have three pairs of true leaves, thin out your seedlings to the strongest one.

Mature size: Allow one foot between plants. Plants will grow up to two feet tall.

Water: Water deeply once per week if outside. It may need two or more shallow waterings per week inside.

Sun: Full sun but can tolerate partial shade.

Cuisines: Italian, American

Maintenance: Six hours of sun or more per day is best. If you want to focus on leaf growth, pinch off the top of the main stem after the first six weeks of growth to encourage the side stems to grow leaves.

Warm or Cool: Warm

Flavor: Spicy

Annual or perennial: Annual

Recipes and uses:

- Italian recipes are an easy way to go
- Basil whipped cream to top lemon shortcakes
- Add basil to your green smoothie
- Use as a sandwich topping to replace your lettuce
- Infuse the basil flavor into olive oil for sauces and dressings
- Mix basil with tonic water and gin for a refreshing cocktail
- Other flavors that are great with basil: watermelon, strawberry, blackberry, shrimp, coconut milk, beef broth, tomato

Blue basil

This kind of basil can grow over six feet tall. It thrives best in tropical climates. It's native to Africa and South Asia. You can use it like other types of basil. But, it can also be cooked like greens.

How to plant: The only way to grow blue basil is to propagate it from cuttings. It doesn't produce seeds well. Cut stems with four or more sets of leaves. Place the cuttings in water for 14 days to develop new roots. Change the water every two days. Once the roots develop, you can plant the new shoot.

Mature size: This shrub can grow over six feet tall and three feet wide.

Water: Once per week is sufficient

Sun: Full sun

Cuisines: This is a hybrid of a basil native to Uganda and Tanzania. But it's a fusion ingredient and is used in fusion dishes.

Maintenance: Pick off the top leaves on the stems to encourage the plant to bush out. Prune your blue basil at the end of the growing season. In spring, remove dead branches.

Warm or Cool: Warm

Flavor: Spicy, like sweet basil, with hints of thyme and cloves

Annual or perennial: Perennial

Recipes and uses:

- A refreshing homemade soda with sparkling water, blue basil simple syrup, and cucumber
- Make a unique blue basil and lavender jam for your French toast
- Top grilled chicken and peaches with your blue basil jam above
- Blend into a green curry with cilantro, cumin, shallots, pepper, and lemongrass
- Pour this curry over steamed clams
- Blend chopped leaves and garlic into mayonnaise to top sandwiches
- Other flavors that pair well with blue basil: strawberry, lemon, crab, chili, watermelon, peanuts, rice

Thai basil

How to plant: Thai basil is best started from seed. Start seeds about four weeks before the beginning of your growing season. After that, slowly introduce them to their final environment over the next two weeks.

Mature size: This plant grows about 1.5 feet tall. It needs about 12" of space around each plant.

Water: A good watering once per week is sufficient.

Sun: Full sun

Cuisines: Thai, Vietnamese

Maintenance: Pluck the first few leaves off the stems to encourage bushiness. Remove the flower stalks as they appear if you want more leaf growth.

Warm or Cool: Warm

Flavor: Anise and a bit spicy

Annual or perennial: Annual

Recipes and uses:

- Stir-fry with ground chicken, peppers, onions, and soy sauce; any meat of your choice really

- Wilt fresh basil leaves into your fried rice or sauteed vegetables
- Add to your salad blend and top with a ginger-soy dressing and orange slices
- Braise chicken thighs in coconut milk, basil, and peas
- Make a basil-lime ice cream
- Basil cheesecake topped with blackberries
- Other flavors that pair well with Thai basil: potatoes, blueberries, raspberries, chocolate, balsamic vinegar, avocado, corn, eggplant

Lettuce leaf basil

This plant is a wonder. Sometimes the leaves can be as big as your hand. And they taste great. I like to use it like lettuce. For example, my BLT becomes a BBT. Three leaves will completely cover a slice of bread. It likes the same conditions as sweet basil. But it deserves a call-out because it's an awesome cultivar.

Bay Leaves

The Turkish and California varieties of bay leaves are the ones you'll encounter most often. Both develop sturdy leaves with pointed ends. The California variety has longer and thinner leaves and has a stronger flavor. You'll notice that fresh leaves are a shiny green on top. The underside is a bit lighter. Because these leaves are tough, they freeze well.

Primarily used in "low-and-slow" dishes that will simmer for a long time. The leathery leaves need time to release their flavor. Most cooks remove the leaf before serving. Fresh leaves are great in teas when steeped for about three minutes or added to a stew with about 20 minutes of cooking time left. Otherwise, the flavor may become too strong.

How to plant: Cut off a 3" branch from an existing tree. Remove the leaves from the bottom ⅔ of the branch. Dip the branch in rooting hormone and then into soil. It will root in about three weeks.

Mature size: Up to 50 feet when mature, but can be kept as small as two feet with pruning. Use this plant to shade others since it likes full sun and grows tall. Allow six feet between plants.

Water: Drought tolerant when established. Water deeply once per week. Allow six feet between plants.

Sun: Full sun

Cuisines: American, Chinese, French, Indian, Mexican, Spanish, and Thai, among others.

Maintenance: Fertilize every two weeks when young. Prune in late winter to shape, to remove damaged areas and suckers that grow at the plant's base.

Warm or Cool: Warm

Flavor: Spicy, bitter, and astringent. Similar to mint or eucalyptus.

Annual or perennial: Perennial

Recipes and uses:

- Bay leaf tea is tastier than you think. It's a must-try
- Bay leaf is a must in Mexican pozole
- Add bay leaves to simmer away in your pot of beans
- Mix bay leaves with anise and orange peel to make a Chinese-inspired beef noodle soup
- Vaca Frita is a Cuban dish of shredded flank steak seasoned with bay leaf, onion, garlic, and lime
- Make a caramelized butter with bay
- Other flavors that pair well with bay leaves: beer, paprika, rosemary, sage, chicken, potatoes, crab, shrimp

Bee Balm

Bee balm or wild bergamot is fragrant and attracts pollinators to your garden. At the same time, the crushed leaves repel mosquitos. That's reason enough to grow this plant. But it's also great in the kitchen. The leaves can be used as a replacement or addition in dishes that call for oregano or mint. The flowers are great in salads and as a garnish. Use both the flowers and leaves to make a fragrant tea or to season a lamb or fish dish.

They grow up to four feet tall, so plant these against a fence or in the middle of your bed if you don't want them to shade other plants. That said, you can also use this plant to shade your more delicate herbs in the hot afternoon sun if needed.

How to plant: Plant from seed in the spring or fall. The seeds need light to germinate. Bee balm prefers moist–but not soggy–soil, so cover nearby soil with mulch.

Mature size: Plants can get up to four feet tall. Space plants at least two feet apart.

Water: Prefers it moist. When the plant is young, water deeply. Water at least once per week once established.

Sun: Full sun but can tolerate partial shade. May wilt in the hottest of climates.

Cuisines: Native to North America

Maintenance: Mold and mildew can be a problem, since it likes wetter conditions. Thin leaves to increase airflow and keep the canopy dry. Cut off dying flowers if you want to encourage more blooms. But you can also let the flowers develop into seeds, which your local birds will love. Cut the plant back to two inches tall in the fall. It will regrow next year.

Warm or Cool: Either

Flavor: Spicy and a bit bitter. Minty, similar to oregano.

Annual or perennial: Perennial

Recipes and uses:

- Use bee balm to make a flavored vinegar or tea
- Use this flavored vinegar to make a bee balm vinaigrette
- Sprinkle over a fresh fruit salad
- Use as a substitute for oregano in pasta
- Add to your tomato sauce for a zesty kick
- Lots of people add bee balm to bread
- Other flavors that would pair well with bee balm: basil, parsley, chives, onions, garlic, mint, thyme, lemon

Betony

    This beautiful herb produces tasty leaves and beautiful pink flowers. People use it because of its calming effect. It's a perennial that will readily self-seed and spread once established.

How to plant: This is an herb that grows well in pots. Betony seeds need to be cold-stratified. Then start the seeds indoors about one month before your growing season begins. Don't cover the seeds with dirt, since they need light to germinate. Keep the seeds moist until they sprout. Make sure the room where you keep the seeds is above 60 degrees. Transplant seedlings when they get three inches tall.

Mature size: About two feet tall and about 12 inches wide.

Water: Water twice per week during the first year. Once per week is good after that.

Sun: Partial shade

Cuisines: English

Maintenance: You don't need to prune betony. Just remove dead flowers to keep the plant healthy.

Warm or Cool: Warm

Flavor: Similar to black tea

Annual or perennial: Perennial

Recipes and uses:

- Use in earthy tea blends with bee balm, orange peel, and yarrow
- Make a milk tea with honey and betony leaves
- Toast the leaves to make a smoked tea
- Flavor a boiled egg with smoked betony leaf tea
- The leaves are great wilted into a soup, especially veggie soup
- Add betony to a true herb salad with cucumbers
- Vanilla bean and betony panna cotta
- Other flavors that would pair well with betony: cinnamon, venison, lamb, seasoned pork sausages, butter, chocolate, berries

Borage

Borage, or starflower, makes beautiful blue flowers that attract lots of pollinators. People use them as a garnish in all kinds of salads, soups, and other dishes. They are great in desserts when used raw. Or, you can candy them. Both the leaves and the flowers are edible. But, select the younger leaves to use raw because they are less fuzzy.

Borage is also known to repel pests. Put it in areas with black flies or even the dreaded tomato hornworm. So, maybe you want it near your beans or tomatoes. Because it gets tall, you should consider the shade the plant will offer when mature. It's a great companion plant for strawberries. Maybe you plant it so that it shades your delicate strawberries or other plants that don't want much afternoon sun.

How to plant: You can plant borage from seed in early spring as soon as the ground is about 50 degrees. Or, if you live in a warm area, plant in the fall when high temperatures don't exceed 100 degrees. If you want to start your plants earlier, start them inside or in a greenhouse.

Borage is a superb source of GLA (gamma-linolenic acid), which helps to combat cancer. Borage is highly toxic to cats and will also cause dogs problems. But, it's not a problem for humans when eaten in small doses.

Mature size: Allow 12" between plants. Borage grows up to three feet tall.

Water: Water every few days when the plant is young. Once a week is sufficient when the plant is established.

Sun: Full sun, but can tolerate partial shade.

Cuisines: European

Maintenance: Remove dying flowers to encourage more flowering. You can pull the plant up at the end of the season, but before going to seed, if you plan to plant something else in that space next year. Otherwise, you'll have lots of new seedlings in that same location next year. Their seeds are also known to germinate in compost piles if not removed or heated to unviability. About 140 degrees will kill any seeds you don't want to sprout.

Warm or Cool: Cool

Flavor: Bitter leaves. Tastes like cucumber.

Annual or perennial: Annual

Recipes and uses:

- Borage lemonade
- Borage, pea, and mint soup
- Cucumber and borage flower salad
- Watermelon and borage flower salad
- Candied borage blossoms
- Spicy chili noodles with borage flowers
- Other flavors that would pair well with borage: bee balm, cilantro, pineapple, scallops, tarragon, watercress, white wine, vodka

Calamint

Use Calamint the same way you would regular mint. It will be less potent because it contains less menthol. So, it won't overpower the way regular mint can in dishes.

How to plant: Start seeds early in the growing season in temperate areas. Plant the seedlings outside in the middle of the growing season.

Mature size: One foot of space is sufficient. It will grow about one foot tall.

Water: Tolerates drought well. It's a great option for xeriscaping.

Sun: Full sun

Cuisines: Italian

Maintenance: Cut the plant back to half its size at the end of the season. This will encourage new growth.

Warm or Cool: Warm

Flavor: Minty, like spearmint

Annual or perennial: Perennial

Recipes and uses:

- Roasted artichoke hearts in cream sauce with calamint
- Calamint and mushrooms are a classic combination
- Make a calamint simple syrup to flavor ice teas and desserts
- Crusted scallops with calamint and peas
- Calamint pesto with basil
- Tomato salad with calamint
- Other flavors that would pair well with calamint: chocolate, citrus, mangoes, dairy, strawberry, feta cheese, garlic

Carrot Leaves

You probably don't think of carrots as an herb, but you should. Carrot leaves are as flavorful as parsley, tarragon, or cilantro. Don't waste them. They are especially tasty in pesto. You can use them as a salad green too. Put them in a soup or stew for flavoring. Add them to mashed potatoes or pasta. Or put them into an omelet.

Maybe you grow carrots already in another part of your garden. Now you have another reason to grow them. Sometimes, you can find carrot greens on top of the carrots at the store. But they won't be nearly as fresh as the ones you grow. And that makes a difference with carrot tops. They are frilly and delicate. So, they get mushy and rot really quickly. Use them as soon as you can once the carrot is uprooted.

You can harvest carrots every three or four weeks. When you pick a group, you can just resow with new seeds throughout the growing season. They can also be planted very densely. So, it's an herb you can have in abundance all season long.

Carrots are biennial, which means that they live for two years. In the second year, the plant produces flowers and then seeds. At this point, the root isn't as crisp. But the blooms are very beautiful, tasty, and edible.

How to plant: You can grow carrot tops from scraps. Put chopped off carrot tops into a shallow container of water. When you see new growth and roots, they are ready to go in soil. To grow from seed, plant seed ¼ deep and cover with a bit of soil.

Mature size: Carrots only need three inches between plants. The tops can get up to a foot tall.

Water preferences: ½ gallon per every 18 plants.

Sun: Full sun

Cuisines: European, American, French

Maintenance requirements: Keep seedlings moist. Put ½ gallon of water on plants after that. Pull weeds when the ground is wet so as not to disturb the carrot roots.

Warm or cool: Cool

Flavor: Sweet and spicy. Similar to parsley.

Annual or perennial: Biennial

Recipes and uses:

- Saute the greens with sesame oil, onions, and garlic

- Carrot top pesto

- Spread carrot top pesto over butternut squash cubes or cauliflower

- Carrot top soup with ginger

- Pulse with yogurt and garlic for a quick sauce

- Throw into a roasted root vegetable salad with beets, parsnips, and carrot root

- Other flavors that would pair well with carrot leaf: bacon, basil, chicken, chives, ginger, mint, rosemary

Catmint

Both catmint and catnip produce a chemical that attracts cats. But catmint also makes a great tea. It's also quite beautiful in bloom.

How to plant: Plant from seeds or divided plants early in your growing season.

Mature size: Give plants one foot of space between each other. It will grow about eight inches tall.

Water: Once per week should be sufficient.

Sun: Full sun to partial shade. It likes shade from the hot afternoon sun.

Cuisines: Dutch

Maintenance: Add mulch to keep the soil moist. You can pinch the top stems when plants are a few inches tall to help them get bushier. You can divide the plants every two years. This plant may attract cats, but much less so than catnip. But you'd do well to put it in an area where their visits aren't a problem. Catmint develops many more flowers than catnip and will likely attract pollinators too.

Warm or Cool: Cool

Flavor: A mild version of mint

Annual or perennial: Perennial

Recipes and uses:

See the recipe ideas under calamint

Catnip

How to plant: Catnip grows well in containers and can be planted indoors and outdoors. Catnip seeds require stratification in the freezer and soaking, each for 24 hours. Then plant the seeds ⅛" deep in the soil. They should germinate in fewer than 20 days. If you don't want to go through these steps, buy live plants.

Mature size: Give plants at least 18" of space between them. It will grow a little over three feet tall if not cut back.

Water: Water it twice per week when first planted. Then, you can reduce it to every two weeks once the plant has established itself.

Sun: Full sun

Maintenance: Make sure there's sufficient room for cats to enjoy the plant without damaging others nearby. They will probably roll around in the plant, keeping it pruned back. Catnip can become invasive if not trimmed regularly.

Warm or Cool: Cool

Flavor: Minty

Annual or perennial: Perennial

Cuisines: Feline! But it's edible by humans in small doses too.

Recipes and uses:

See the recipe ideas under calamint

Celery leaf

This is my favorite herb, hands down! I use it in everything that I can. Celery leaves were used a lot in early American cooking. Today, we primarily want the stalks. But, I think you are missing out on the best part if you don't use the leaves too.

For anything where you use parsley, you can use celery leaf. You can also use it as a substitute for cilantro. So, if you're one of those people who doesn't like cilantro but that loves tacos, try adding a bit of celery leaf to your taco the next time.

You can grow regular celery and harvest those leaves. Most people will have plenty of leaves with just normal celery. But there's another variety called cutting celery, leaf celery, or Chinese celery that's grown primarily for its leaves. It grows back quickly after cutting and is quite hardy.

It's true that celery is available in almost every grocery, but it's hard to find many leaves on these. Manufacturers cut the leaves off to save space since most people want the stalks. But maybe you can find whole stalks with leaves at the farmers' market.

How to plant: Celery is great in containers. You can regrow celery from the base you've cut off a full-grown plant. Just sit the base in a shallow container of water. It should start to regrow in about a week. When it has roots, you can put it in the soil. This is a great way to keep lots of leaves around. The stalks won't be perfect since this is from a cut- off plant. But we're most interested in leaves here, so this should work just fine.

Celery takes a long time to grow. Start it three months before you will plant it outside. Soak the seeds overnight in warm water. The next day, spread the seeds out over your seed starting kit. Don't cover with more soil. Leave them bare and cover the container with plastic wrap or a top to keep in the heat. When they sprout, give them plenty of light. You can put the seedlings in bigger pots when they are two inches tall. A week before you want to plant them, water them a bit less and put them outside for a few hours each day to get them used to the outdoors.

Mature size: About 1.5 feet tall. Plant at least six inches apart.

Water: Water celery every day when temperatures are more than 70 degrees. Every other day is fine when temperatures are cooler.

Sun: Full sun

Cuisines: American, Italian, French

Maintenance: Celery likes enriched soil and plenty of sun and water. It doesn't need pruning or much maintenance. But you can tie the plant stalks together so that the interior parts get less sun. This makes them sweeter.

Warm or Cool: Cool

Flavor: Bitter and a bit sweet. The leaves taste like celery with a hint of anise.

Annual or perennial: Biennial

Recipes and uses:

- Use as a garnish over any pork dish: sausages, stews, roasts
- Celery leaf is a must in any true herb salad
- Homemade cream of celery soup is so much better than canned
- Celery leaf vinaigrette will brighten up any salad
- Sparkling celery soda will cheer you on a sweltering day
- Make a homemade celery salt to season all of your meats
- Other flavors that pair well with celery leaf: apple, cucumber, dill, parsnip, fennel, shellfish, lovage, tarragon

Chamomile

There are two common varieties of chamomile: German and Roman. Roman chamomile has the classic apple fragrance that gave the plant its name. Chamomile means ground apple in Greek.

If your soil is not amended, German chamomile may do better in your garden. The German version smells more like grass and grows tall. It doesn't hug the ground, as you might guess, based on the meaning of the word chamomile.

You can use both in your tea. But I think the Roman is more versatile.

Most people use the sunny-looking centers in teas. But you can use chamomile to flavor any liquid you want. A recipe that I really like involves infusing chamomile flavor into dairy. That recipe is chamomile panna cotta. It is delicious.

Just because chamomile is a common tea ingredient doesn't mean you can't get creative. Think about using it in vinegar, alcohol, and oil. You can also use the petals directly. In my opinion, they would be great in baked goods, especially shortbread cookies. You can add them candied or plain to your favorite sweets.

How to plant: It grows great in containers and outdoors. Sow seeds directly after the last frost or at the very beginning of your growing season. You can also divide existing plants and plant them elsewhere in your garden.

Mature size: Roman chamomile won't get taller than six inches. Plant at least six inches apart.

Water: Once per week is sufficient.

Sun: Full sun, but can tolerate some shade.

Cuisines: European, American

Maintenance: Roman chamomile grows quickly and spreads fast. It reaches full bloom in just 10 weeks. You can divide the plants to keep them in check.

Warm or Cool: Either

Flavor: Roman chamomile is slightly sweet, like honey, with hints of apple.

Annual or perennial: Roman chamomile is a perennial.

Recipes and uses:

- Chamomile tastes great in any dish with apples or honey
- Make chamomile syrup to use in desserts
- Chamomile panna cotta
- Chamomile and lavender lollipops
- Sticky honey and chamomile chicken wings
- Chamomile and honey rice porridge for breakfast
- Other flavors that would pair well with chamomile: chocolate, lemon, celery, fennel, thyme, orange, pork, pumpkin, rosemary

Chervil

It's also known as French parsley. But chervil means rejoicing in Greek. And you will rejoice when you harvest it from your garden. It's not the easiest to grow. It's hard to germinate, doesn't like to be transplanted, and grows slowly. But the flavor is worth the effort.

Since chervil has a delicate flavor, you should use it in lighter dishes. Omelets, potatoes, rice, light chicken, white fish dishes, or salads would all work with chervil. But, it can be a great substitute in any dish that calls for parsley. This is an herb best enjoyed when fresh rather than dried.

Because it doesn't like to be transplanted, put the seeds where you expect the plant to live for that season. If you really enjoy this herb, plant new seeds every two weeks to harvest it all season. Chervil likes full shade. So, use it to fill up your garden's low–light areas.

How to plant: Grows well in containers and in beds. It's an excellent choice for growing indoors. But make sure your container is deep enough for chervil's long taproot. It can grow up to eight inches long. Chervil doesn't like to be transplanted. Plant seeds ¼ inch deep and cover with soil. Make sure there's no threat of frost before planting if you live in a temperate area.

Mature size: Space plants at least six inches apart. The plants will grow up to two feet tall.

Water: Water very well. Prefers moist soil. But be careful not to over water it.

Sun: Partial or full shade

Cuisines: French

Maintenance: Give chervil some shade if the weather gets too hot. It can also bolt when the weather gets warm. Frequent trimming will help keep it bushier and help prevent bolting.

Warm or Cool: Cool

Flavor: Slightly bitter and peppery. It's like a cross between parsley and anise.

Annual or perennial: Annual

Recipes and uses:

- Make an omelet filling with salmon, chervil, and cream cheese
- Chervil and lobster ravioli
- Make chervil oil for vinaigrettes
- Chicken liver pate with chervil and cognac
- Sauteed leeks, mushrooms, and chervil
- Chervil is an excellent garnish over any creamy soup
- Other flavors that would pair well with chervil: basil, fennel, lovage, duck, mint, peas, thyme

Chives

They look like vibrant green tufts of grass with fluffy purple or white flowers on their ends. They are so cute that some people use them as decoration. You can eat both the leaves and the flowers. The stalks are hollow tubes and are very delicate.

Chives will attract pollinators. Bees especially love chive flowers. But, they will keep away lots of other pests. So, that's another reason to plant them.

The word chives comes from Latin and means onion. And that's kind of what they taste like. So, use chives where you want just a hint of onion kick. Chive greens make a lovely garnish on most any dish. They are most often used fresh rather than cooked. Heat will render them even milder. So if you're putting them on a warm dish, do so at the end.

Cut the stems at the base when harvesting. This will also encourage new growth. The stems with flowers are not good to eat.

Your chives will be ready to harvest 60 days after you plant the seeds. If you let the flowers go to seed, they will spread throughout your garden.

How to plant: Chives grow well in containers. Plant the seeds about ¼" deep. Then, use just enough soil to cover them. They will sprout within three weeks. They are relatively maintenance-free.

Mature size: Plant at least six inches apart. They may grow up to a foot tall.

Water: Water at least once per week. If it rains regularly where you are, you won't need to water them.

Sun: Full sun to partial shade

Cuisines: American, French, Chinese, Vietnamese, Thai

Maintenance: There is no need to thin out your chives during the growing season. They will die back in fall and winter, but don't worry. They will come back. Divide the plants every two years.

Warm or Cool: Cool

Flavor: Savory and spicy. Similar to onions, but milder.

Annual or perennial: Perennial

Recipes and uses:

- A Chinese-inspired scallion pancake
- Sprinkle chives over a stir-fry with pork, chili oil, and peanuts
- Fry your chives in oil to get flavored chive oil
- Drizzle your chive oil over roasted potatoes, cauliflower, or an omelet
- Make a chive oil salad dressing
- Make a cream cheese and chive dipping sauce
- Other flavors that would pair well with chives: basil, green beans, dill, sweet potatoes, squash, tarragon

Cibola

This plant is also known as hart's tongue fern. The fiddleheads are a delicacy. If you see one in the wild, it indicates that you're in an ancient woodland. So, treat this plant with care. It will provide green foliage all year round if it doesn't freeze where you are.

How to plant: Since this is a fern, it grows from spores, not seeds. So, buying a live plant or making a division from an existing one is easier. This is a common houseplant and works well indoors. You can plant them outdoors as well. As with all ferns, they need a lot of water. They like rocky areas. But you may also want to put some mulch around them to help retain moisture.

Mature size: It will grow to 1.5 feet tall and 1.5 feet wide if given the right conditions.

Water: Keep the soil moist all the time. You may need to water it several times a week.

Sun: Partial to full shade

Cuisines: American

Maintenance: This is a great plant for humid bathrooms. It likes very high humidity areas. Avoid areas with more than three hours of sun per day. Remove any dry leaves.

Warm or Cool: Cool

Flavor: Similar to asparagus, vegetal

Annual or perennial: Perennial

Recipes and uses:

- You must cook these before eating them
- Boil in salted water and serve with butter
- Stir-fry with ginger, anchovies, black bean paste, and garlic
- Serve in a warm salad with edamame and goat's cheese
- Serve in pasta with garlic
- Roast in the oven with potatoes and rosemary
- Other flavors that would pair well with Cibola: carrots, goat cheese, ham, chives, lobster, peas

Chicory

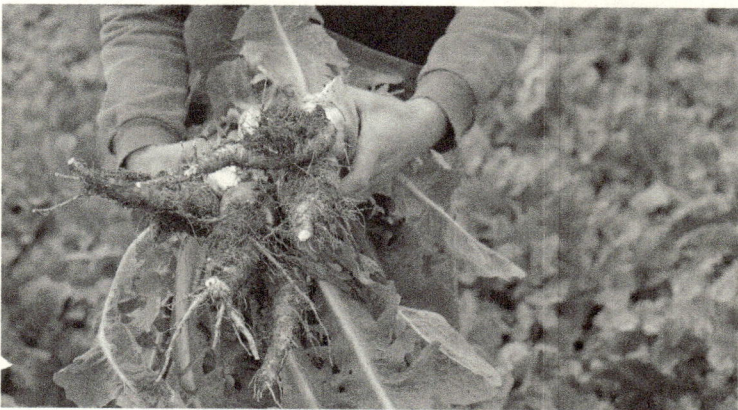

You can eat the leaves, flowers, and roots of this plant. It's been a staple of human food consumption for thousands of years. This is different from the chicory you see at the store. The leaves look more like dandelion than gourmet lettuce. Use it the way you would other bitter greens.

How to plant: Plant seeds ¼' deep in the soil at the beginning of the growing season. Sprouts will emerge within three weeks.

Mature size: Flower stems grow up to three feet tall. Give one foot between each plant.

Water: Once per week is sufficient.

Sun: Full sun

Cuisines: Italian, California, New Orleans Creole

Maintenance: You will need to pull up the whole plant, including the roots, if you see an individual growing where you don't want it. Snip off dead flowers to prevent reseeding.

Warm or Cool: Cool

Flavor: Bitter, similar to dandelion

Annual or perennial: Perennial

Recipe and uses:

- Saute with bacon and onions as a side dish
- Mix this saute into a warm bowl of buttery polenta
- Chicory and fava beans are a classic combination
- Serve raw chicory leaves with anchovy dressing
- Serve a chicory salad with blue cheese and pear
- Chicory with roasted pork in sweet and sour sauce
- Other flavors that will pair well with chicory: figs, lemon, orange, radishes, thyme, walnuts

Cilantro

We talked about French parsley. Well, cilantro is also known as Mexican parsley, Chinese parsley, Indian parsley, and sea parsley. When you're using the seeds, this plant is called coriander.

The entire plant is edible. The root is the most flavorful part, but the least used.

It's one of the most used herbs in the world. But not everyone likes it. Some people have a smell receptor that makes cilantro taste like soap. About 10% of people have these smell receptors, including Ina Garten and Julia Child. Fewer people have these smell receptors in places where cilantro is used a lot.

Cilantro is probably one of the most versatile herbs around. It's great in almost any dish you can think of: meat, fish, potatoes, rice, beans, and more. It's particularly good in spicy dishes because it's slightly cooling.

This is another herb that is best eaten fresh. Add it at the last minute, just before serving, if you put it on a hot dish.

If you live in a hot place, succession planting can help you keep lots of cilantro around. Just put in a few seeds every few weeks.

How to plant: Soak seeds overnight before planting. Plant seeds about ¼ inch deep in early spring or in the beginning of your growing season. Thin seedlings when the plants have their first true leaves.

Mature size: Plan for one plant per square foot. This plant can grow up to two feet tall. Cilantro is also great in pots.

Water: Water your cilantro plants once per week.

Sun: Full sun, but will bolt if it gets a lot of sun in a hot climate.

Cuisines: Mexican, Thai, Vietnamese, Indian, Chinese, North African

Maintenance: If you let it, cilantro will self-seed. Mulch around the plant

Warm or Cool: Cool

Flavor: Sour, herbaceous, and refreshing. Some people describe it as a combination of parsley and lemon, a great combination!

Annual or perennial: Annual

Recipes and uses:

- Cilantro is delicious in Vietnamese-style beef noodle soup
- Cilantro is a staple flavor in Pad Thai
- Pico de gallo is a Mexican salsa that includes cilantro
- Cilantro-garlic grilled shrimp
- Cilantro ranch
- Corn chowder with cilantro
- Other flavors that pair well with cilantro: avocado, coconut, cucumber, lamb, lentils, mint, yogurt

Dock

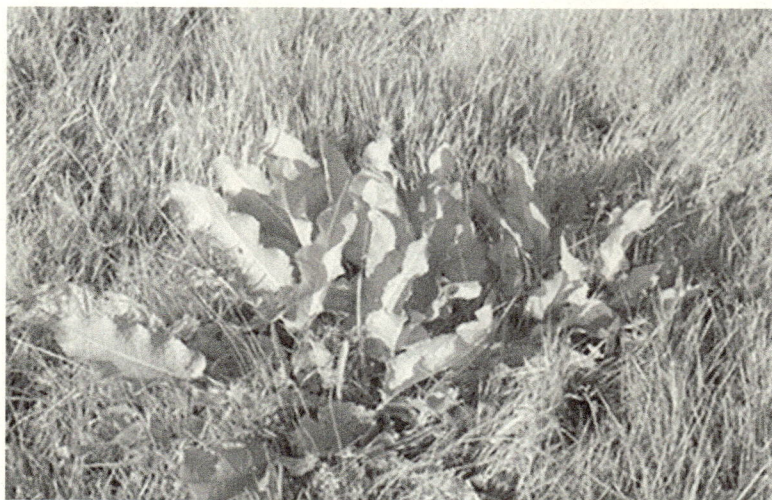

You may see dock growing out in the wild. If so, try it. The leaves are long and narrow, which makes it easy to get a roll that will hold food tightly. So, a traditional use is to wrap butter and cheese in these leaves. You'll get that characteristically sour flavor to infuse and keep the food in your desired shape.

You can stuff dock leaves with anything you want. A mix of ground lamb and rice would be delicious. The options are endless.

If you wait until the fall, you can also enjoy the seeds and the root. You can continue to enjoy the roots before the ground freezes. After that, you can store the root. It's a great plant year-round.

Leaves that get a lot of sun or that are very big will be more bitter. So, you may want to harvest younger leaves if you're not going to cook them.

How to plant: You can start growing dock almost any time of the year. If you put the seeds out in the fall, you'll get a nice patch in the spring.

Mature size: Broadleaf dock grows to 1.5 feet tall. Curly dock can grow up to five feet tall when you include the flower stalk.

Water: Once a week is fine. This plant likes moisture but can tolerate dry conditions because of its long taproot.

Sun: Full sun to part shade

Cuisines: Balkans, Mediterranean

Maintenance: Docks can grow in all types of soil. So, they can easily take over if you let them reseed.

Warm or Cool: Cool

Flavor: Sour

Annual or perennial: Perennial

Recipes and uses:

- Puree your dock leaves with chicken stock for a zesty soup
- Stuff your dock leaves with rice, ground pork, and herbs
- Steam your cod in dock leaves with dill, pepper, and butter
- Dock gratin with potatoes and peas
- Bake dock leaves until they are crispy for a snack
- Lacto-ferment the leaves for a probiotic slaw
- Other flavors that would pair well with dock: bacon, chicken, chard, cream, garlic, salmon, tomato

Dill

Dill comes from a Norwegian word. It means to soothe. It's an illustrious name because I find that to be very true of dill. There are so many soothing classic recipes with dill: dill pickles, tzatziki, tartar sauce, and ranch dressing.

Imagine the deliciousness of ranch dressing from scratch! It's not that hard to do. It's basically sour cream, buttermilk, dill, and other spices. Dill is great in other sauces, too, especially sauces with a bit of acid.

Dill is native to Southeast Asia, so you can find it in those cuisines. For example, in northeastern Thailand, it's used in curries that don't have coconut milk. It's also great with fish, chicken, rice, potatoes and eggs. Just a small bit of dill really can lift a dish.

Dill will bring lots of beneficial insects to your yard. But don't plant dill near fennel. They can pollinate each other.

This is another herb that reseeds easily. The leaves aren't as flavorful after flowers develop. But the flowers are also edible and tasty.

How to plant: Dill doesn't like to be transplanted because it has a long taproot that's easily damaged. Sow it from seed. Plant seeds ¼ inch deep in the early spring or the beginning of your growing season. In ten days, you should start seeing sprouts.

Mature size: Plant one dill plant per square foot. It can grow up to three feet tall.

Water: Water your dill plants once a week.

Sun: Full sun, but can handle shade. Plant in shady areas if you live in a hot place.

Cuisines: Russian, Indian, American, Turkish, Persian, Thai

Maintenance: Cutting the leaves at the top will help the dill stay bushy. Prune regularly during your growing season. Dill will bolt when temperatures get over 80 degrees. Some shade in the afternoon will help it continue to produce leaves. Cutting the flower stalks will also help the plant continue to produce leaves.

Warm or Cool: Cool

Flavor: Sweet and grassy, with a slight anise flavor. Similar to fennel.

Annual or perennial: Annual

Recipes and uses:

- Add a spring of dill to your salmon sushi
- Dilly mashed potatoes
- Chilled cucumber dill soup
- Dill pickle soup is a warm and sour version that is super tasty
- It's not tartar sauce without dill
- It's also not ranch dressing without dill
- Other flavors that pair well with dill: carrots, chicken, lemon, mint, peas, seafood, tomato

Fennel

Fennel is considered a vegetable and an herb. It's related to carrots. But the bulb grows above ground rather than underneath, like its orange cousin. It's also closely related to dill.

It's known for its frilly, feathery leaves and its distinctive licorice flavor. But the whole plant is edible. And I highly recommend using all of it. Grilled fennel root will change your life! The seeds or fruit are also used for flavoring. Let the plant overwinter to give the plant time to bloom and produce its fruit. You can use the stalks as a replacement for celery.

Most recipes you see will mention the bulb. But here, we are interested in the leaves. They are great as a garnish and add flavor in hot and cold dishes. Think pestos, stocks, curry, and salad dressings. You can even add them to your favorite vegetable dish. Fennel and apple are also a classic combination. And any dish with dill would also be tasty with a sprig or two of fennel fronds.

How to plant: They grow well from seeds planted at the very beginning of your growing season. Soak your seeds for a day before planting. The seeds should germinate in under two weeks. You can grow fennel in pots, but they will require a lot of space.

Mature size: Space plants about six inches apart. They will grow up to six feet tall.

Water: Water daily when potted. Water weekly if in the ground.

Sun: Full sun

Cuisines: California, American, Chinese, Italian, Indian

Maintenance: Fennel takes three months to develop a mature bulb. But you'll be able to enjoy fronds just a few weeks after you plant. Fennel is a perennial. But, most people start from scratch with new plantings each year. Regular fertilizing will promote more leaves.

Warm or Cool: Cool

Flavor: Herbaceous and spicy with a strong anise flavor.

Annual or perennial: Perennial

Recipes and uses:

- Use fennel fronds like dill
- Pasta in fennel cream sauce
- Roasted tomatoes and fennel roots with fronds for garnish
- Fennel and pork is a classic combination

- Sausage fennel stuffing

- Puree roasted onion, fennel bulbs, and carrots into a soup. Top with fronds

- Other flavors that would pair well with fennel: apples, chicken, dairy, garlic, gin, lemon, seafood

Lavender

There are over 40 kinds of lavender. But French and English are the two common varieties you'll encounter in gardens. English lavender does better in cooler places. French is better in warmer climates.

Pollinators love lavender flowers. But, it repels deer and cats. In fact, it's toxic to pets. But humans love it. We have used it for over 2,000 years. The Egyptians and Romans used it. There are even references for lavender in the bible. But today, we mainly associate it with French cooking.

You'll see lavender in sweet dishes more than savory ones. Lavender shortbread, lemonade, butter cookies, and ice cream are all popular uses. But you can use it with savory dishes too. It's great with sweet potatoes and chicken. You can also put the leaves in salads or use them as garnish.

You can eat both the leaves and the flowers as is. But, a more common way to use lavender is to infuse its flavor into dairy, alcohol, vinegar, oil, and, of course, water. From there, you can add a bit of the infusion to any dish you like.

How to plant: Lavender is difficult to grow from seed. Buy starter plants or propagate from cuttings. Lavender does well in containers that are large enough.

Mature size: Only grow one plant per square foot of your garden. When fully grown, lavender can get up to three feet tall.

Water: Drought-tolerant once established. Once per week is sufficient when first planted. Watering every two to three weeks is sufficient for mature plants. If you want to encourage more flowers, water once weekly when you notice buds.

Sun: Full sun

Cuisines: French, Spanish, English

Maintenance: Lavender needs more water during its first year. It's drought-tolerant after that. Avoid planting in wet areas or reduce watering if your soil holds water easily. Remove the dead flowers to encourage more to grow. Give the plants some cold protection if you live in a cold place. The roots of plants in pots will also need cold protection, since the soil in the pot will cool faster than the ground. Trim lavender in the spring in cool climates. Prune your lavender plants in the fall in hot climates.

Warm or Cool: Warm

Flavor: Sweet and floral. It's like a cross between rosemary and mint.

Annual or perennial: Perennial

Recipes and uses:

- Lavender chocolate chip ice cream

- Lavender flowers, blueberries, and granola over yogurt

- Lavender lemonade

- Honey lavender roasted almonds

- Lavender honey for your tea

- Lavender sourdough or scones

- Other flavors that would pair well with lavender: apples, figs, marjoram, orange, rosemary, thyme, vanilla

Lemon Verbena

Lemon Verbena tastes like citrus more than most other herbs. It's great to have it around for its fragrance. As the leaves get crushed by activity in the garden, they release their scent. The same is true in a salad. Imagine a fruit salad for breakfast with this fragrance.

Lemon verbena tea is a very common recipe. But you can make syrups with it and use them in any dish you like. You can use both the leaves and the flowers.

This plant is native to the Amazon rainforest. So, it likes warm and humid weather. Keep this in mind when caring for lemon verbena. If the roots get too cold–below 40 degrees–the leaves will drop.

How to plant: You can start with a seedling, root, or cutting. Plant it when temperatures are a bit warmer. This means in late spring in a cool place or in about late September in a hot one. It grows well in containers.

Mature size: Lemon verbena grows up to three feet tall in containers. Its height in the ground will vary based on your climate. In warm areas, it can grow up to 15 feet tall. Allow for two feet between each plant.

Water: Water a few times a week, just enough to keep the soil barely damp.

Sun: Full sun

Cuisines: Peruvian

Maintenance: In cool places, grow in pots that can be moved to a location that won't freeze.

Warm or Cool: Warm

Flavor: Sour and a bit sweet, like lemons

Annual or perennial: Perennial

Recipes and uses:

- Lemon verbena tea is the classic use
- Lemon verbena vinegar
- Lemon verbena bread
- Lemon verbena sugar
- Chop and add to fruit salad
- Use with raw fish dishes like ceviche
- Other flavors that would pair well with lemon verbena: apricots, basil, berries, dairy, honey, peaches, thyme

Lemongrass

You may see lemongrass referred to as Malabar grass, silky head, or barbed wire grass. People have used its stalks as far back as 5,000 years ago. It's regularly used to make teas, season stews, and for medicinal purposes. It's also a common treatment for high blood pressure in the Caribbean.

Lemongrass contains citronella. It's the same ingredient used in commercial bug repellants. So, adding lemongrass to your garden will help repel mosquitoes, flies, fleas, and ticks. It masks the smells these animals use to find you and bite. But it's also toxic to dogs. So, be careful if your pets are roaming around this plant.

Harvest when the plant is about one foot tall and 1/2 inch in diameter. That's the sweet spot between having enough herb to use and it not being so big that it becomes tough. Never harvest more than ⅓ of the plant at one time.

You can cut the white shoot into chunks and add it directly to your food. But it's also possible to infuse liquids with lemongrass flavor. Similar to the way many people use herbs such as lavender and roses, infuse water, oil, vinegar, alcohol, and dairy with lemongrass. You can then add those infusions to other recipes to get the citrusy goodness of lemongrass.

How to plant: Lemongrass grows well from seed. Plant them about ¼ inch deep. The seeds usually germinate in less than two weeks. When the seedlings are three inches tall, thin them down to one plant per two square feet. But, the seeds are often hard to find. You'll probably have an easier time finding live plants. Lemongrass can thrive when propagated as well. Plant clusters of five to six bulbs to grow a healthy stand. Lemongrass grows well in pots too. Just be sure to put the pot in a very sunny spot.

Mature size: Give plants at least two feet between each other. Lemongrass can grow up to four feet tall.

Water: Water thoroughly once per week.

Sun: Full sun

Cuisines: Indian, Cambodian, Chinese, Thai

Maintenance: Lemongrass likes it warm and humid. If your area is like that, your plants may grow and even become invasive. Give the plant a big chop in the spring. But you can also trim the tops throughout the year when the plant becomes unruly. You may want to wear long sleeves, pants, and gloves when handling this plant. The leaves can leave little cuts on your skin. The plant may die back during winters in cooler climates. But it should come back the next year. You can also plant a few bulbs in a pot inside to keep growing this herb all winter long.

Warm or Cool: Warm

Flavor: Sour, like a combination of lemon and ginger

Annual or perennial: Perennial

Recipes and uses:

- Grilled chicken with lemongrass glaze
- Stir-fried skirt steak with lemongrass
- Tom Kha is a soup with coconut milk and lemongrass
- Red curry with lemongrass
- Fish balls in chicken and lemongrass broth
- Tumeric lemongrass ice cream
- Other flavors that would pair well with lemongrass: anise, basil, chives, clove, peanuts, pork, shellfish

Lovage

It kinda looks like flat-leaf parsley, and the leaves have a similar texture. But it tastes more like anise or fennel. That might sound intimidating. But in reality, there's a ton you can do with this herb.

I love lovage because it's another herb that gives you a ton of leaves. Put it in your salad blends. It's an especially pleasant addition to true herb salad blends.

Lovage is also great in mayonnaise-based salads such as potato salad, egg salad, chicken salad, or tuna salad. It pairs well with fresh spring flavors such as spring peas and asparagus. Add it to dishes with duck or seafood. Or, add a bit to any sauce or dressing that has parsley in it. The sky's limit once you get some experience with this herb.

How to plant: Plant seeds directly in soil early in your growing season. Just lightly cover the seeds. You can also start seeds indoors 1.5 months before your growing season starts. Transplant the seedlings when they have two sets of true leaves. You can also succession plant seeds every two weeks and harvest the young leaves each month.

Mature size: Lovage can grow to over five feet tall. Give each plant three feet of growing space if you keep them for several years. But you can also plant them 18" apart for annual sowings.

Water: Water twice per week to help keep the soil moist.

Sun: Full-sun

Cuisines: English

Maintenance: The leaves will be more bitter if you let lovage dry out. Add mulch to help the soil stay moist at all times.

Warm or Cool: Cool

Flavor: Anise, like a cross between celery and parsley

Annual or perennial: Perennial

Recipes and uses:
- Use as a substitute for parsley or celery leaf
- Use it as a garnish in your bloody mary
- Lovage, prosciutto, and shallot frittata
- Lovage and pistachio pesto
- Lovage and garlic vinaigrette
- Chilled green pea and lovage soup
- Other flavors that would pair well with lovage: apples, chicken, clams, dill, lemon, canned tuna, vinegar

Marjoram

Marjoram and oregano are related. And they have similar flavors. Add marjoram to any dish that will taste good with oregano in it. It makes a great kitchen window plant that you can snip when you want a fresh hit of herbaceousness. Use both the flowers and the leaves.

Here's another idea for using marjoram. If you want a lighter, more complex tomato sauce, use yellow tomatoes and add marjoram. Yellow tomatoes tend to have a milder flavor than their red cousins. And marjoram is like a lighter version of oregano.

You can harvest marjoram 60 days after planting or when the plant is four to six inches tall. Add marjoram to your garden to attract pollinators. It's also an excellent ground cover. You can use it to help keep weeds down.

How to plant: Soak seeds overnight to help them germinate. Start your seeds inside about two months before the start of your growing season. Transplant the seeds into larger pots when the plants are strong enough to handle the move. And make sure that you water it regularly right after planting the seedling. Marjoram grows well in pots.

Mature size: Leave at least 12 inches between plants. They grow up to two feet tall.

Water: Marjoram is drought-tolerant. But water liberally at least once weekly, or you may notice some wilting.

Sun: Full sun

Cuisines: French, Greek, Turkish, Early American

Maintenance: Trim off buds to encourage more leaf growth. You can prune again in the middle of the season to remove the woody parts of the plant. Marjoram can develop rhizomes to spread out. It also readily reseeds. That's another reason to keep it trimmed. Marjoram doesn't like it much below 70 degrees. So, you may want to move it indoors when temperatures get cool.

Warm or Cool: Cool

Flavor: Spicy, like oregano, but more subtle.

Annual or perennial: Marjoram is an annual in cool locations and a perennial in warmer ones.

Recipes and uses:

- Use as a substitute for oregano
- Pea shoot and marjoram salad with radish vinaigrette
- Honey-roasted sweet potatoes or squash with marjoram butter
- Fried hand pies stuffed with cheese, tomato, and marjoram
- Marjoram orange creme brulee
- Lemon cake with honey marjoram cream
- Other flavors that would pair well with marjoram: beans, carrots, dill, lemon, olives, peas, rabbit

Marigold

As herbs, marigolds are grown for their blooms. Like roses and saffron, you can create a tea to flavor dishes. For example, marigold-scented flan. But you can also eat the petals directly on salads.

If you're not familiar with how to use this herb, think of it the way you do tarragon. It has a similar flavor and makes an excellent substitute. You can also use marigolds as food coloring. They will add a lovely yellow or orange hue to your food in addition to their distinctive flavor.

How to plant: You can start marigolds from seeds up to eight weeks before your growing season begins.

Mature size: From six inches to three feet, depending on the variety.

Water: Once per week is sufficient.

Sun: Full sun

Cuisines: Indian, Mexican

Maintenance: Cut off dead blossoms to encourage the growth of new buds. Marigolds are great self-seeders, so beware if they start to encroach on other plants.

Warm or Cool: Warm

Flavor: Sour with notes of tarragon

Annual or perennial: Cempasuchil, the most common type of edible marigold used in Mexican cuisine, is an annual. But you can find both annual and perennial varieties of marigolds.

Recipes and uses:

- Add marigolds to your chicken broth for extra tang
- Chicken salad with marigold, dill, and lovage
- Tea: marigold, bee balm
- Cocktail: marigold syrup, smokey mezcal, sparkling water
- Marigold vinegar
- Seared scallops in marigold butter
- Other flavors that would pair well with marigold: apricots, beets, green beans, peas, crab, grapefruit, mint

Mint

Let me start by saying that the mint granita recipe in this book is crazy good. It's a bit Southern American, a bit Italian. It's kinda rustic and kinda elegant. Once you've tried it, it will become part of your dessert roundup.

Mint is pretty common in sweet foods. Sweet tea, mojitos, and mint ice cream are all mint-based staples. But you can use mint in savory foods too. Mint sauce is excellent with lamb. Or add some mint to your fresh peas with feta. It's also great on roasted green beans, brussel sprouts, or a green salad. You can also infuse mint into liquids like other herbs.

There are over 600 types of mint. But most people plant peppermint. It's the flavor we most associate with mint. It's in gum and toothpaste, and mouthwash.

There are also lots of traditions associated with mint. In some places, it's the flavor of Christmas. In others, it's the flavor of the tea you drink in the morning or to meet friends. It's a social flavor. And, in the southern US, it's a flavor of summer. So, there's lots of nostalgia associated with this herb.

Most people want to use the leaves. But you can eat the flowers too. They will also attract butterflies, hummingbirds, bees, and other pollinators. But remove them to help the plant focus on leaves if that's your goal.

How to plant: Plant mint in the earliest part of your growing season. Sow the seeds ¼ inch deep. The seeds will germinate in under two weeks. Thin out the seedlings when they have four true leaves. Mint is aggressive. So, it's best to grow it in its own bed or pot. You can also use it as a ground cover.

Mature size: Plant four mint plants per square foot. It usually grows to two feet tall.

Water: Water thoroughly once per week.

Sun: Full sun

Cuisines: Mint is truly an international ingredient. American, Southern American, Indian, Vietnamese, Lebanese, Iranian, Greek, Cuban, Morocco, English.

Maintenance: Mint will out-compete most plants for space and nutrients. Thin it back as needed.

Warm or Cool: Cool

Flavor: Sweet, numbing, and cooling or refreshing.

Annual or perennial: Perennial

Recipes and uses:

- Watermelon and mint salad is now a classic
- Mint and peas are another classic
- Eat mint and peas whole, as a puree, or as a soup
- Cucumbers and mint are also a classic, with feta

- Mint-mango iced tea

- Mint Julep with whiskey

- Roasted zucchini or winter squash with mint

- Other flavors that would pair well with mint: berries, carrots, dairy, lentils, lime, radishes, thyme

Mizuna

This is a Japanese mustard green and has a similar intense flavor. It's great in salad blends. But pickling is also a traditional way to use it as well. You can overwinter mizuna in a greenhouse. But most people plant it as an annual.

My experience is that mizuna is less likely to bolt than other salad greens, so it's good to have around for that reason too. This is a cut-and-come-again plant, so you can have fresh mizuna for quite some time during your growing season.

How to plant: Plant seeds ¼" deep a few weeks before the growing season starts in your area. The seeds will germinate in about a week. Or you can start seeds indoors about one month before the beginning of your growing season. Give indoor seedlings four weeks to mature before planting them outdoors.

Mature size: They get up to one foot tall. Give plants four inches between them.

Water: Once per week is fine for Mizuna.

Sun: Part sun

Cuisines: Japanese, Californian

Maintenance: You can plant seeds every two weeks for new young plants. You may need some shade in the hottest part of the year.

Warm or Cool: Cool

Flavor: This is a bitter green with a flavor similar to turnip greens.

Annual or perennial: Annual

Recipes and uses:

- Make sure you use this as a salad green in summer when everything else has bolted
- Mizuna salad with apples and celery leaf
- A simple saute with onion and bacon
- Stir sauteed mizuna into risotto or stewed beans
- A simple saute with soy sauce, garlic
- Add the greens to a southeast Asian-style beef broth with anise
- Add peanuts, tofu, and chili oil to make a meal from the soy saute above
- Other flavors that would pair well with mizuna: daikon, dill, eggs, ham, mustard sauce, pears, vinegar

Nasturtium

I love having nasturtium around because you can use so many parts of it, and it's super easy to grow. The leaves, seeds, and flowers are all awesome. It also self-seeds really easily. So once you plant it in a good spot, it will regrow every year.

It's known for its distinct peppery flavor. So, I'll throw in a few nasturtium leaves or petals whenever I want a peppery kick. They are outstanding in salads. You can also chop the leaves up finely and use them in fresh sauces and salad dressings.

The only way I know to use the seeds is to pickle them. That makes the hard shell soft and edible. I put some in a beet, orange, and fennel salad, and they were delicious.

There are about 80 species of flowering nasturtium. It's in the same family as watercress. That makes sense, as both have a note-worthy peppery taste. They are also related to the brassicas: cabbage and broccoli.

If you have problems with pests eating your cabbage, you can put nasturtium in front of them to use as a sacrifice. But I'd probably just buy cabbage at the store and try to save my nasturtium. Cabbage is pretty cheap, and nasturtium is a delicacy, in my honest opinion.

The two most common nasturtium varieties in gardens are dwarf nasturtium and garden nasturtium. These are a blend of the original plants that hail from the Andes Mountains in Peru. The plants were first brought to Spain in the 16th century. Later, they crossed the Atlantic again and arrived in North America.

How to plant: You can start nasturtium seeds indoors about a month before planting them. Put your seed starter or pot in a sunny window and make sure the soil is always moist. It grows well in containers and pots.

Mature size: About one foot tall. This plant likes to spread out, usually no more than one foot. But, plants will put out runners and reseed to fill any bare ground. They make great border plants. On the other hand, they can be invasive if not tamed.

Water: Once a week should be fine. Adjust the amount of time you water as the weather warms. Aim for getting the soil wet down to six inches deep.

Sun: Full sun

Cuisines: Southern American, Peruvian, Chilean, Mexican. Often used as a garnish for fine dining dishes in many cuisines.

Maintenance: Cut back areas that are damaged or where flowers have died. If it's dry or very hot where you live, consider adding mulch to keep the ground moist. You don't need to fertilize nasturtium.

Warm or Cool: Cool

Flavor: Peppery, spicy

Annual or perennial: Annual

Recipes and uses:

- One of my favorites for spring salads of leafy greens
- Pair this peppery salad with grilled beef
- Nasturtium butter would also be great on beef or venison
- Pickle the leaves with other herbs to make a peppery sauerkraut
- Nasturtium vinegar
- Add some hot peppers to the nasturtium vinegar to make a peppery hot sauce
- Other flavors that would pair well with nasturtium: beans, gin, lemon, olives, pork sausage, whiskey, yeasty bread

Oregano

If you plant oregano in the right conditions, you'll have so many leaves that you can use it as a salad green. If you're a person that doesn't like bland lettuces, you should consider this option. An oregano leaf-based salad next to your steak, or salmon or pork, or even lobster will change the way you eat dinner forever! At least, it did for me.

In ancient Greece, farmers let their cows graze in oregano fields so their meat would be tastier. But now, it may be most associated with Italian food. We sprinkle it on pizza and put it in pasta sauces. But it's much more versatile than that.

Obviously, you can use the leaves. But the purplish flowers are also edible and quite tasty. I also like to use the woody stems. When they are dried, you can use them for smoking. You can even use them for kebab skewers if they get big enough.

Oregano and mint are related. So, consider adding oregano to any savory dish where you'd typically use mint. It's also great in sauces like pestos and chimichurri. Or just mix some into regular old mayonnaise to put on a sandwich for lunch.

How to plant: You can start seeds or a cutting one month and a half before planting it outdoors. Make sure the soil is at least 70 degrees before planting your seedlings. If planting indoors, make sure there's plenty of sun. A south-facing window is best.

Mature size: They won't get any taller than two feet tall and two feet wide.

Water: Oregano is drought-tolerant. Let the soil dry between each watering.

Sun: Full-sun

Cuisines: Ghanaian, Greek, Nigerian, Mexican, Italian, Turkish, Californian

Maintenance: To keep the plant bushy with leaves throughout the season, pinch off the top two leaves of each stem. But be aware that this will reduce your number of flowers as well. Prune back woody areas that no longer produce leaves in early fall or just before the plants go dormant. This usually happens after most of the flowers have died back for the year. This is also a good time to fertilize. You can do a big chop of very large branches in winter.

Warm or Cool: Cool

Flavor: Herbaceous, slightly bitter

Annual or perennial: Perennial

Recipes and uses:

- Many West African Jollof rice recipes include oregano

- Oregano and garlic pesto will change your life

- Put this garlic and oregano pesto on grilled chicken

- I often use oregano as the base for my true herb salads

- Oregano in tomato sauce is classic

- Make oregano butter in a skillet

- Baste your next steak with oregano butter

- Oregano is an ingredient in Mexican mole

- Other flavors that would pair well with oregano: beans, ground beef, lamb, paprika, rosemary, potatoes, pork sausage

Parsley

Most people grow parsley for its leaves. But the flowers and seeds are edible too. There are two common types of parsley: curly leaf and flat leaf. You can largely use them interchangeably, especially if you're blending or chopping them very finely. But, there are a few pros and cons for each.

Curly has a milder taste that most people say is better than flat. So, it's great in fresh salads and sauces. Tabbouleh and chimichurri are better with curly parsley to my palate. And if you're making Cuban food, some people will say curly is the best option. The same is true for parsley with seafood. Traditionalists may argue that the more delicate flavor of curly is better with delicate proteins like light fish or scallops.

Curly parsley is also a more lush-looking garnish because of its height on dishes. You can also fry curly parsley leaves and make a crispy snack or garnish. Curly is also bouncier when you chew it. But it's also a bit coarser to chew than its flat cousin. Overall, there are more pros than cons to curly parsley.

On the other hand, flat is easier to clean. There are no areas for dirt to hide. It also works better as a chopped ingredient in delicate cooked sauces; think cream sauces. It's also the preferred parsley for European dishes.

So, it's really up to you which to use. Grow a bit of both side-by-side and see how much you use of each. Right now, I have flat parsley chopped up and ready to go in my fridge. But after thinking about it and after writing this section, I'm considering the change to curly.

How to plant: This is a great herb for your outdoor garden or pots. Parsley seeds take a long time to germinate, up to one month. So, be patient or buy seedlings. You can start parsley in containers or directly in the ground. Plant your seeds ½" deep. It can tolerate a light frost. So, you can plant seeds up to a month before the last spring frost outside or up to two months early indoors.

Mature size: No more than two feet tall and no more than six inches wide.

Water: Once per week is fine, but make sure the soil stays moist.

Sun: Prefers full sun but can tolerate some shade.

Cuisines: French, Italian, Spanish, Middle Eastern, Cuban, American

Maintenance: Parsley doesn't like to dry out. So, add mulch to keep the soil moist. Adding fertilizer will help the plant with leaf production.

Warm or Cool: Cool

Flavor: Herbaceous and mildly bitter

Annual or perennial: Annual

Recipes and uses:

- Add parsley to your cold bean salad: black-eyed peas, tomatoes, onion, and parsley

- Cold pasta salad with tomatoes, onions, and parsley

- Cherry tomato salad with parsley

- Make herb rice with parsley and other herbs

- Garlic parsley butter

- This butter would be good on chicken, beef, or fish

- Other flavors that would pair well with parsley: bulgur wheat, carrots, lovage, parsnips, shellfish, thyme, zucchini

Peas

Most people probably don't think of peas as herbs. But they are. And they can be used that way. They make superb microgreens. You can even saute pea shoots.

For me, pea shoots, watercress, and purslane can be used similarly in cooked dishes. They are excellent with fresh pasta if you blanch them lightly in salted water. A cream cheese ravioli with blanched herbs is a perfect use for pea shoots.

You can also use them in heartier, meatier dishes. Pair pea shoots with fattier meat such as pork shoulder or duck thighs.

You want to just clip and use the ends of the pea fronds. These are the most delicate and will have the best texture.

How to plant: Plant peas directly in soil as soon after the start of the growing season as you can, but after the threat of extreme weather has passed. Or you can plant peas in containers and grow them next to a sunny window. Keep the area moist until they have sprouted. You want to harvest the shoots when they are about six inches tall.

Mature size: Mature bush pea plants can grow up to three feet tall. But you want to harvest your peas for herb usage sooner.

Water: Water them at least once weekly if there's no snow or rain.

Sun: Full sun to part shade

Cuisines: Chinese, Japanese, English, American

Maintenance: You will generally need to harvest and replant for shoots every three weeks to one month. If you let them grow longer than that, they will be fibrous.

Warm or Cool: Cool

Flavor: A blend of peas and spinach

Annual or perennial: Annual

Recipes and uses:

- Sautee pea shoots lightly with garlic and olive oil or soy sauce
- Mix the sauteed pea shoots into risotto, polenta, or a bean stew
- Don't miss out on a pea shoot salad in the spring with radishes

- Spicy pea shoot kimchi

- Pea shoot pesto

- Pea and pea shoot soup

- Other flavors that would pair well with pea shoots: arugula, basil, chicken, mint, lobster, rosemary, scallops

Purslane

For me, the number one reason to have purslane around is the crunch. I love chewing the snappy leaves and stems fresh. Purslane is pleasure food. Yes, I know I'm talking about a green leafy thing here. But that's how I feel.

It's got a fairly neutral flavor. But it's a bit salty, naturally, which I also love. It doesn't need much seasoning since it's a bit savory already.

To me, it's best used fresh, like in a salad. But you can use it similarly to the way watercress is used. For example, wilt it slightly and use it in pasta with artichokes, peas, and butter. If you decide to cook it all the way through, pair it with a fatty cut of pork. The first dish of that sort that comes to mind for me is pork ribs with purslane.

How to plant: Plant seeds directly in the ground early in your growing season. You can also root cuttings in water and plant these once the roots are one inch long.

Mature size: It will grow about six inches tall, on average. Give plants eight inches of growing space.

Water: Twice per week in the spring and the fall. Two to three times per week in the hottest times of the year. If it doesn't freeze where you live, water it once every two weeks during the cold season.

Sun: Full sun

Cuisines: Indian, Persian, Uzbek, Greek, Mexican, Turkish, South African

Maintenance: Because it's a succulent, purslane is drought tolerant, but the leaves are crunchier if it receives adequate water.

Warm or Cool: Warm

Flavor: Salty and sour

Annual or perennial: Annual

Recipe and uses:

- Steamed and in a simple lemon vinaigrette

- Fresh in a summer salad

- Corn, purslane, and roasted tomato salad

- Lacto-fermented pickle to make a healthy slaw

- Lebanese bakleh is purslane and onions baked in puff pastry

- Verdolagas is a Mexican recipe of purslane, tomatoes, and spices you can use to stuff tortillas

- Other flavors that would pair well with purslane: avocado, toasted bread, lemon, nuts, eggs, stone fruit, vinegar.

Radish

I prefer radish leaves when they are small. Microgreens or sprouts are just delicious and best used fresh. Add them to your salad blends, to the top of sandwiches, or in fresh sauces like pesto.

As the leaves mature, they are best cooked. Add them to your milder sauteed greens such as spinach, kale, chard, collards, or cabbage. Adding some radish greens to your creamed or buttered spinach will give it a nice kick. Radish is known for its peppery kick. That's why people enjoy them.

Larger varieties of radishes, such as daikon, mature in 50 days. You can use the leaves on these too. But, most people are focused on the roots for the larger varieties.

The smaller varieties of radish roots, such as the red French breakfast variety you see in groceries, can mature in about 30 days. So, you can have herbs from this kind of radish on hand throughout your growing season. Each time you harvest a section of the roots, plant a few more seeds there to keep the harvest going.

You can also plant seeds every two weeks and harvest just the microgreens. This is possible no matter the variety of radish. So, choose the variety that has the best flavor for you.

Growing microgreens is a great indoor gardening project. It's a great way to start herb gardening if you're new to it. You can grow microgreens in a sprouter, seed starter, or just a regular pot with dirt.

How to plant: Plant groups of seeds ½" deep and one inch apart. If you want the roots to mature, thin the seedlings after one week.

Mature size: The smaller varieties will grow to about 4 inches tall.

Water: Water once per week

Sun: Full sun when the weather is cool. Full shade if you live in a hot place or at the height of summer in a temperate place.

Cuisines: French, Californian, Korean, Chinese, Southern American

Maintenance: Hot weather and little water will create weaker plants. Consider moving your radish operation indoors in the hottest months if you don't want to or can't provide adequate shade.

Warm or Cool: Cool

Flavor: Spicy and peppery

Annual or perennial: Annual

Recipes and uses:

- Radish butter is lovely in spring
- Radish salad is also great in spring
- Serve radish salad alongside fried foods, like fried pork chops
- Roasted radishes with herbs are also lovely

- Roasted pork tacos with radish

- Sliced radish in pork broth with Szechuan peppercorn and noodles

- Other flavors that would pair well with radishes: anchovies, basil, chives, cucumbers, dill, mint, seafood

Roses

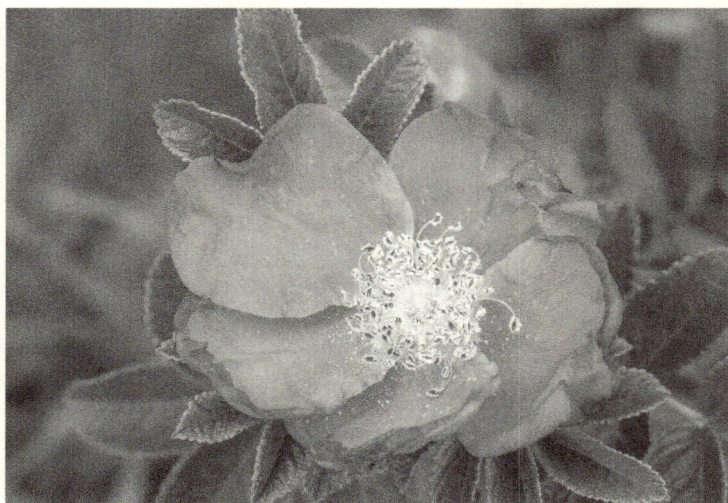

All roses are edible as long as you don't put poison or toxic chemicals on them. But, the varieties with the most fragrance will also have the most flavor. This is important when choosing your rose variety as an herb.

Many commercial varieties sold for gardens are bred more for impressive-looking blooms rather than impressive-smelling blooms. So, I recommend planting a wild, local variety. Most wild roses only have one layer of petals. So, they don't look as magnificent as commercial varieties. Still, they smell much better, attract more local pollinators, and will taste better.

You can enjoy the petals fresh in salads. But, the most common way to use roses is to infuse a liquid with their fragrance. You can infuse alcohol, water, dairy, and oil to use in any dish where you want a floral kick.

Even though most people focus on the petals, the fruit, the leaves, and even the young shoots are edible. So roses are quite a versatile plant to have as an herb.

How to plant: Rose seeds need to be fooled into thinking they went through a winter before they will germinate. Typically, this means putting them in a cold and moist place for at least two months. Your refrigerator will do. The next step is to let the seeds warm to at least 70 degrees while still moist.

You should start to see some germination after about a month. But not all of your seeds will germinate. Store-bought seeds will germinate better than ones you harvest yourself.

There are a lot of steps to sprout your own seeds. This is not for beginners. I would not even encourage this for intermediate gardeners unless there's a variety you can't grow another way.

I think the best way to plant roses is with young plants. These will be bigger than sprouts and seedlings. You want mature but small plants, at least a year old.

To plant your new rose bush, remove it from the container and loosen the root ball a bit. Put fertilizer in your hole. Then finally, place the bush.

Mature size: Rosebush sizes can vary. Some miniature rose buses only grow eight inches tall. The tallest varieties can grow more than 50 feet tall. So, your spacing depends on the type of bush you buy. Your best bet is to look at your label or ask the clerk at your local garden center.

Water: The first year, water your roses at least twice weekly. Add one more day of watering if you notice them wilting a bit. Once per week should be sufficient after that, except in the hot summer or if you live in a very warm place. In both of those cases, stick to two times per week.

Sun: Full sun

Cuisines: Persian, Indian, French, Greek, Turkish, Middle East, North Africa

Maintenance: Prune roses early in the growing season to promote new flower growth. Fertilizing is important for any flower that you want to bloom copiously. This includes roses. So, fertilize at least twice per year.

Warm or Cool: Warm

Flavor: Sweet, somewhat like strawberries. The texture of the petals can be a bit satiny in your mouth.

Annual or perennial: Perennial

Recipes and uses:

- Rose petal jam is delightful on pancakes or French toast
- Make rose petal sugar
- Make rose milk to have a rose latte
- Pistachio rose cream tart
- Rose mint ice tea
- Rose and harissa is a great combo with paprika, chili, and olive oil
- Other flavors that would pair well with roses: almonds, honey, lemon, rosemary, saffron, strawberries, vanilla

Rosemary

Rosemary plants can live up to 20 years. So, put this plant in a space that can be occupied for a while. Rosemary is an evergreen, so you can have fresh herbs in the middle of winter.

This woody herb is quite versatile. You can use it in sweet and savory dishes. I can't think of a food that doesn't taste good with rosemary. It's also easy to grow once established and is drought-tolerant. So, it's a good one for beginners.

You can chop up the leaves and sprinkle them directly on your food. But you should also try infusing liquids with rosemary's flavor, so oil, alcohol, dairy, and water. You can also use the wood for smoking, as kebab skewers, or sprinkle the flowers over your food as a garnish.

How to plant: You can grow rosemary indoors. But it does much better outside. Just barely plant seed under soil, as shallow as you can. If using seedlings, make sure your hole is the same depth as the container that the rosemary was in before.

Mature size: Up to six feet tall, if given the space, and two feet wide.

Water: Rosemary is drought tolerant. You can get away with watering it once per week. Make sure the soil is dry to the touch before watering again. Rosemary also likes its leaves wet, so put some water on them each time you water. If you notice droopy leaves or stems, water deeply, but not necessarily more frequently. If the tips of the leaves turn brown, add a bit less water next time.

Sun: Full sun. Rosemary does not like shade.

Cuisines: French, Spanish, Italian, American, Greek

Maintenance: Plants in sunnier and hotter areas will have a more intense flavor. You can prune the plant after the flowers have died back for the year. Don't prune more than a third of the plant in a single year.

Warm or Cool: Warm

Flavor: Kind of like a mix of pine and mint.

Annual or perennial: Perennial

Recipes and uses:

- Chicken and rosemary are a great combo
- Rosemary butter over potatoes is serious comfort food
- Use woody rosemary stems to grill scallops
- Put rosemary in all of your bread, sweet and savory
- Rosemary is great with herbaceous drinks like gin
- Sprinkle rosemary over stewed beans
- Puree those beans with rosemary to make a delightful dip
- Other flavors that would pair well with rosemary: apricots, carrots, dairy, grapefruit, honey, lavender, lemon

Saffron

Yes, it can be expensive. But you can also grow it.

I like saffron in anything with lamb. So, rice pilaf with ground lamb, saffron, and pine nuts is a winner for me.

Saffron ice cream is one of my favorites as well. When I lived in San Francisco, there was a store called Bombay Creamery. I believe it was on Valencia street, in the Mission. That's where I first saw this idea. And it stuck. I make saffron ice cream about once a year now.

It's also great with oatmeal. Some might think using an "expensive" ingredient like saffron with oatmeal is a waste. But I think combining a "high" ingredient with a "low" one is an exciting contrast. It's a different kind of balance in food.

Each saffron flower only makes three strands of this herb. But that's enough for one serving. So, plant one plant for each serving of saffron you want to use that year. They don't take up much space and look stunning. So I say to give it a go.

Infuse the saffron flavor in three tablespoons of water for every three stamens. Use this saffron tea to flavor any dish you like.

How to plant: Saffron can be grown indoors with the right conditions. Plant bulbs in four-inch grooves in the summer or fall.

Mature size: Give each bulb four inches of growing space.

Water: Water once per week while growing. After you have pulled the stamens, stop watering the plants.

Sun: Full sun

Cuisines: Indian, Persian, Moroccan, Spanish

Maintenance: When the flowers have bloomed the following fall, pull the orange strands or stigmas from the flower using tweezers. This is the saffron. It's best to pick it the same day each flower opens.

Warm or Cool: Warm

Flavor: Floral and sweet

Annual or perennial: Perennial

Recipes and uses:

- Let's start with saffron rice with pine nuts
- Saffron rice pudding is an easy next step
- Paella almost always includes saffron
- Steamed clams with saffron herb butter
- Indian gulab jamun are fried dough balls in saffron rose syrup
- Saffron and chicken is a world-class combo
- Other flavors that would pair well with saffron: anise, carrots, cloves, fennel, orange, prunes, tomatoes, vanilla

Sage

Not all varieties of sage are edible. Common sage is what you'll see in gardens most often. White sage, which is native to the southwestern US and northern Mexico, is also edible. You might also come across Pineapple sage, which grows in Mexico and Guatemala.

Sage's fuzzy leaves are rarely used raw. But, the flavors are often infused into liquids. Sage-flavored teas and cocktails are very popular now. But you can also infuse oils and dairy. Sage is also quite tasty in honey.

Use this versatile herb in baked goods, stews, sauces, or gravies. Many people out there wouldn't dream of chicken or turkey gravy without sage. When you prune your sage, don't throw the woody parts away. Use them as skewers or in your smoker.

Fried sage leaves are great crumbled over a dish as a garnish or just eaten as a snack. Sage flowers are also edible. You can also use them as a garnish in salads or over cooked dishes. But be sure the pieces aren't too large. They'll be overpowering if they are too big.

Because sage is a perennial, plucking a few leaves in the dormant season is okay. Just don't pull too many so it can flourish next season.

How to plant: Sage grows well in containers, but only outdoors. Young sage plants are best planted when the weather is cooler, usually in early spring or late fall. If you're using seeds, plant them two weeks before the last frost date or two weeks before the beginning of the growing season where you live. Ideal soil temperatures are between 60 and 70 degrees Fahrenheit. It may take up to six weeks for seeds to germinate. But, some early sprouts may appear after just three weeks. That's why most people use live plants rather than waiting. Sage requires patience.

Mature size: Common sage will get about two feet tall and two feet wide at its max.

Water: Sage is very drought-resistant. It can survive a long time without water. Watering once per week is more than enough.

Sun: Full sun

Cuisines: English, Italian, American, Native American, Mexican

Maintenance: Prune your sage plants after the flowers die back for the season. If your sage is in a pot, make sure it has excellent drainage. Sage likes very dry conditions. If your plant is no longer producing leaves, consider replanting. This may happen around year three.

Warm or Cool: Grows well in warm and cold climates.

Flavor: Like a mix between pine and mint. It can be drying in your mouth if the pieces are too large. So, cut them smaller or cook them.

Annual or perennial: Perennial

Recipes and uses:

- Sage and poultry is a delicious combo
- Sage-infused brown butter is super tasty
- Sage butter on pumpkin is a fall delight
- Pour this sage butter on gnocchi or other pasta
- Use this butter to make sausage stuffing

- Drink sage and lemon tea on a chilly night
- Other flavors that would pair well with sage: cabbage, egg, honey, orange, mint, peas, pears

Salad Burnet

This is a great herb to use in salads, obviously. You can also use this leaf as a replacement for mint. Use it for all of your summer drinks. Or, put it in your newest herb blend.

How to plant: This herb grows well in containers and in the ground. Start the seeds about a month before the beginning of your growing season.

Mature size: Up to two feet tall. Give the plants two feet between them.

Water: Once per week is sufficient for salad burnet. Keep the soil permanently moist in the summer.

Sun: Full sun to partial shade

Cuisines: English

Maintenance: Remove the flower stalks to encourage more leaf growth. Mulch will help keep the soil moist.

Warm or Cool: Cool

Flavor: Similar to cucumber

Annual or perennial: Perennial

Recipes and uses:

- Perfect for fresh salads
- Use salad burnet with cream cheese to make tea sandwiches
- Use as a replacement for cucumbers
- Burnet and tomato salad with goat's cheese
- Make a burnet martini
- Salad burnet dip with yogurt, chives, and garlic
- Other flavors that would work well with salad burnet: chives, dill, cumin, gin, lemon, parsley, shellfish, tarragon

Shiso

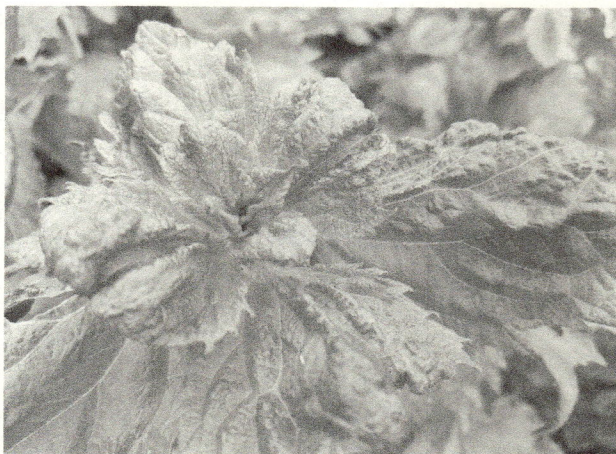

This herb tastes like no other. If you haven't yet, you absolutely must. Some people call it Japanese mint, and it is slightly minty. But, it's also fruity-tasting to me as well.

You can use it in dishes that call for mint. But it's also a good stand-in for tarragon, basil, and even cilantro. It's super versatile.

This is an herb you want to use fresh. The leaves are tough and a bit hairy if not fresh. And my suggestion is to cut it very finely so you don't get too much of the texture when eating it. But don't let that scare you away. This herb is a downright delight.

There are two varieties you're likely to encounter. Red Shiso leaves are a bit tougher. But they add a nice color. The green variety is slightly more delicate. It's my preferred variety to grow.

Use this herb, chopped, in salads or as a garnish. Also, try it for drinks. Shiso lemonade might just change your life. You might also see it in sushi rolls. A pickled plum and shiso sushi roll is killer. It's also excellent with mango.

Ok, let me stop here. I could keep going on forever about this herb….

How to plant: Soak seeds a day before you plant them. Then plant them in soil. You should see some young sprouts in under three weeks.

Mature size: Give plants a foot of space between them. It can grow up to three feet tall.

Water: Water briefly at least two times per week. You want to keep the soil moist at all times. This plant can stand some dryness but does better in moist soil.

Sun: Full sun

Cuisines: Japanese

Maintenance: Pinch off the top leaves to encourage bushier growth. Pinch off the flowers if you don't want to seed save. This will encourage more leaf growth.

Warm or Cool: Warm

Flavor: Minty and herbaceous

Annual or perennial: Perennial

Recipes and uses:

- Great in raw sushi dishes: tuna, salmon, yellowtail
- Shiso rice seasoning: soy sauce, sesame seeds, chili powder, and chopped shiso
- Shiso kimchi
- Watermelon salad with shiso
- Use as an alternative for mint
- Shiso iced tea
- Other flavors that would pair well with shiso: avocado, cucumber, ginger, mango, peach, pork, watermelon

Sorrel

One of my favorite occasions each year is when there's enough sorrel to cook with. Then for me, it's time to make salmon and sorrel. This was the first haute cuisine dish, and it's super tasty. It's basically salmon in a cream sauce with sorrel in it. This is a fun little celebration to mark the coming of spring.

Sorrel is great with fish because it's sour. It's also delicious with other seafood. But you can use it in any dish where you want a sour kick. It's especially nice in salads when the greens are young.

Be careful when cooking it if you have a version of sorrel with a red streak. It can create a bit of a pink hue in your food. So, add it last if you can.

How to plant: Plant seeds directly in soil, either in a container or in the ground. You can plant outdoors as early as two weeks before your growing season starts.

Mature size: Give each plant four inches of space to grow. Sorrel won't grow more than two feet tall.

Water: Water twice a week when young, then once per week when mature.

Sun: Full sun

Cuisines: French

Maintenance: This is a low-maintenance herb and will provide leaves all season. But in my opinion, young leaves taste the best.

Warm or Cool: Cool

Flavor: Sour, it's related to dock.

Annual or perennial: Perennial

Recipes and uses:

- Strawberries and whipped cream with baby sorrel
- Sorrel, crab and avocado ceviche
- Cheesy sorrel, cauliflower, potato bake
- Soup: puree of wild garlic and sorrel in chicken broth
- Sorrel lime mojito
- Grilled scallops and onions with mixed sorrel salad
- Flavors that would pair well with sorrel: celery, eggs, bacon, leeks, lentils, peas, watercress

Spring onions

Maybe spring onions don't come to mind when you think of herbs, but they should. The bulbs and the tubular stems are important flavorings and garnishes. They are great in stir-fries and also pickled. Also, try throwing them on the grill with a bit of olive oil and salt.

If you let the plant grow an additional year, spring onions will develop flowers. The blooms are great as a garnish or to infuse liquids with an onion flavor. They are sweeter and milder than other parts of the plant.

To be clear, all onions qualify as herbs. Everyone around the world uses them as a flavoring. But in this section, I'm referring to spring onions, not green onions. Spring onions have a small bulb at the bottom, unlike green onions.

You can use spring onion leaves as you would green onion leaves in garnishes, sauces, and stir-fries. But you can also roast or grill them. They are also sweeter and less sharp than green onions.

Have you ever had a roasted onion souffle? It's killer. Roasting and grilling caramelize the sugars, making the onions taste sweeter. You can take advantage of this sweetness much more with a spring onion than with scallions. In my opinion, this makes them more versatile than green onions. You get the best of both worlds with this type of onion.

If you only have room for one type of onion in your herb garden, go with springs. I think you'll get much more use out of them.

How to plant: Spring onions are great in containers, indoors and outdoors. Just be sure you have enough light. Plant your seeds about ½" deep at the beginning of your growing season. When you pull the mature plant, put a few more seeds in that area for a continuous harvest.

Mature size: Your spring onions will get about a foot tall. Give each plant four inches of space to mature.

Water: Watering once per week is sufficient.

Sun: Full sun

Cuisines: Most cuisines in the world include spring onions

Maintenance: Spring onions may survive the winter. So, this is a plant you can keep harvesting all year long.

Warm or Cool: Cool

Flavor: Milder, sweeter version of a large white onion.

Annual or perennial: Annual

Recipes and uses:

- Spring onion fritters
- Spring onion and tarragon quiche or omelet
- Beef and spring onion stir-fry with noodles
- Potato and spring onion soup
- Spring onion crab cakes

- Spring onion and shrimp dumplings

- Other flavors that would pair well with spring onions: citrus, cucumber, ginger, mint, mushrooms, seafood, sesame, parsley

Stevia

Stevia is typically used as a natural sweetener. You can chop or grind the leaves and add them to dishes where you want a hint of sweetness. You can use it in hot or cold dishes. Or just snack on the leaves as a treat.

Not all stevia plants will offer the same level of sweetness. If you're buying live plants, test the leaves of the plant you want to buy. If you still taste sweetness after 30 minutes, you've selected a healthy plant. Take that one home. If you get less sweetness than that, keep checking other plants.

This tip also comes in handy when it's time to plant more stevia. If you decide to seed save from your stevia plant, obviously, you'll want to save from the sweetest plant. The same applies if you're growing stevia from cuttings. Take cuttings from the sweetest plant.

Don't let your stevia plant develop flowers unless you are seed-saving. Pinch off the flowers before they bloom. As soon as you even see tiny buds, get rid of them. The leaves lose much of their sweetening power when flowers are on the plant.

How to plant: You can grow stevia in the ground or in containers as a houseplant. You can start seed early, in late winter, or a few weeks before your growing season begins. This plant is native to the tropics. So, don't plant it until well after the threat of frost has passed. You can also take cuttings that are at least six inches long from mature plants. Remove the last few leaves and put the cutting in wet soil for 4 weeks. That should be enough time for it to develop roots. You can then pot it in something bigger or put it in the ground.

Mature size: Up to three feet tall and 18" wide.

Water: Stevia likes to be consistently wet. A constant trickle of water is great for this plant.

Sun: Full sun

Cuisines: Brazilian, Canadian, Chinese, Japanese, Paraguayan

Maintenance: Regular fertilizing will encourage leaf growth. If you notice your plant wilting, it's probably because it's drying out. Stevia is a great candidate for mulch since it doesn't like dryness.

Warm or Cool: Warm

Flavor: Sweet with a hint of licorice.

Annual or perennial: Perennial in warm climates. Annual in temperate and cool ones. Plants won't be as lush in the second year. So, most people just replant every year.

Recipes and uses:

- Steep with your tea blends as a natural sweetener
- Make stevia syrup by soaking leaves in warm water for 24 hours
- Use this syrup in beverages
- Make a stevia extract by soaking leaves in vodka for two days, then reduce it to a syrup
- Use this extract in sauces and liquid desserts, one teaspoon per cup of sugar
- Use one tablespoon of ground leaves for every cup of sugar in baking
- Using stevia instead of sugar can make a recipe keto
- Flavors that would pair well with stevia: It's super versatile. It can be a replacement anywhere your recipe calls for sugar

French Tarragon

French tarragon is actually native to Russia and is part of the sunflower family. But it's the preferred variety in European cooking. This plant has the classic tarragon flavor called for in most recipes.

A cream sauce with tarragon over chicken is a classic. But it's also great with eggs or added to olive oil. It's best to use tarragon as fresh as possible. This isn't an herb to cook in a stew for a long time. Add it at the very end of preparing your dish.

This is one of the more difficult herbs to grow. They don't grow well from seed and don't like temperatures over 90 degrees. So, if that's true for you, put it indoors. Some gardening books will say that you can just offer it shade. This may work some, but getting it out of the heat is a much better idea.

This is one of the most flavorful herbs around. That's why people bother with it, even though it's tough to grow. If you're a beginner or intermediate gardener, enjoy tarragon while you can. But don't feel bad if the plants look bad or die. It's just the way it goes with tarragon. You'll need a few seasons of trial and error to figure out what will work in your space.

The availability of plants is very seasonal. If your plant dies, don't expect to find more until the next season rolls around. I always buy a few just in case something goes wrong.

You may also encounter Russian tarragon and Mexican tarragon. Both have an anise-like flavor and are in the same family as French tarragon. These are heartier and less fussy than the "French" variety. So you can try these if you can't get the French to grow. They'll deal better with more extreme conditions.

How to plant: Buy healthy live plants. This herb rarely flowers or seeds. So, it's almost impossible to grow it any other way except via cuttings.

Mature size: The healthiest tarragon plants can be three feet tall and 15 inches wide.

Water: Water every other day when it's dry out or when the plant is young. Twice per week is sufficient for mature plants in ideal conditions.

Sun: Full sun in temperate climates. Indoors in your sunniest window in warmer places.

Cuisines: French, English, California

Maintenance: If your tarragon starts to bolt in the hot summer months, it will need pruning. Cut off the flower stalks so that the leaves don't become bitter. You can also pinch off the tips of the shoots to encourage branching out.

Warm or Cool: Cool

Flavor: Licorice or anise

Annual or perennial: Perennial

Recipes and uses:

- Add it to mayonnaise for your salads: tuna, chicken, coleslaw, potato
- Put this mayonnaise on fried food: fish, crab cakes, fried pork chops
- Add tarragon to a dish with root vegetables: potatoes, squash, carrot, parsnip
- Mix tarragon with white wine, butter, and maybe saffron for a fragrant broth for seafood
- Classic bearnaise sauce includes tarragon
- Add tarragon to vinaigrettes
- Other flavors that would pair well with tarragon: beans, citrus, eggs, gin, peas, pickles, poultry, strawberry

Thyme

This hearty herb is sometimes grown in the cracks between bricks. When you walk over it, a delightful lemony fragrance is released. Because it's so hardy, it's a great herb for beginners to have around.

Thyme is an evergreen. So, you can pick leaves even in the winter. It's also quite versatile. You can use it in savory and sweet dishes, cooked and cold dishes, and even beverages. In fact, I can't think of a dish where thyme wouldn't be tasty.

Lemon thyme and common thyme are seen most in the garden. Obviously, the citrus notes of lemon thyme are stronger than in the "common" variety. But you can largely grow them and use them the same.

Getting the leaves off the stem is the biggest complaint about thyme. The leaves are quite small and difficult to pluck off with your fingers. An easy way to remove them is to slide your index finger and thumb down the stem. Once you get the hang of it, you can remove thyme leaves faster than many other leaves.

If the stem you're working on is brittle, soak it in water before removing the leaves. Or if you're using the thyme in a stew, you can throw the bunch in, stem and all.

Thyme leaves are small enough that I generally don't chop them. They are garnish size by default, in my opinion.

How to plant: Thyme grows well in pots and indoors. Consider moving indoor plants outside if conditions permit. Plant seeds outdoors just after the last frost or at the beginning of the growing season. The seeds don't need to be buried deeply, just barely covered with soil. Expect some sprouts in a month. Because the seeds take so long to germinate, live thyme plants are a good option too.

Mature size: Plants will get just over a foot tall. Give each plant one foot of space.

Water: Once every two weeks is fine.

Sun: Full sun, but will manage in part shade.

Cuisines: American, Greek, Italian, Indian, Jamaican, Spanish, Turkish, Mexican, Middle East, Morrocan

Maintenance: You can prune the woody parts off your thyme bush in the coldest part of the year. If you get frost where you live, do the chop then. Cut about ⅓ of the woodiest part back yearly until the bush is flourishing again.

Warm or Cool: Cool

Flavor: Citrus or lemony

Annual or perennial: Perennial

Recipes and uses:

- Thyme is maybe the most versatile herb out there. It goes with everything
- Baked apples in red wine and thyme syrup
- Grilled lamb chops basted in thyme butter

- Stuff mushrooms, thyme, and goat cheese in ravioli or an omelet

- Thyme and roasted onion souffle

- Lemon and thyme are a classic combination

- "Italian seasoning" includes thyme

Winter Savory

Savory is the herb you've been missing in your garden. It tastes like a cross between thyme, pine, and mint and is easy to grow. The best time to harvest savory leaves is before the plant flowers. But the flowers are edible as well.

There are two varieties common in herb gardens: winter and summer. Winter savory is a perennial, and summer savory is an annual. The winter variety has more pronounced pine notes. So, people sometimes use it for heartier foods such as root vegetables and goose. And they save summer savory for lighter fowl like chicken. But you can largely use them interchangeably in your cooking. Just adjust your amounts to get the flavor you want.

Because winter savory is evergreen and only needs to be planted once, it's my preference. I love the option of grabbing a handful of fresh herbs even when there's snow outside. And, it's one less thing to plant during the sometimes hectic planting season.

My suggestion is to find the plant at your local garden center and pick a leaf or two. If you like it, add it to your garden. Then, add it to your pots of beans. Savory and beans are a classic combination.

How to plant: Start seeds indoors about a month before the growing season. Don't bury them. Just cover them lightly with soil. They need light to germinate. Seeds should sprout in under two weeks. You can also start savory from cuttings. Use pieces that are at least six inches long. Place the cuttings in potting soil until roots form. Then you can transplant it to its final destination. Cuttings are the most common way to propagate savory.

Mature size: One foot tall by one foot wide

Water: Two times per month is sufficient.

Sun: Full sun

Cuisines: Bulgaria, Romania, Canadian

Maintenance: Pinch savory at the tips of the stems to encourage bushing out. You can then use these trimmings in your food.

Warm or Cool: Cool

Flavor: Herbaceous, like a cross between mint, pine, thyme, and oregano.

Annual or perennial: Perennial

Recipes and uses:

- See the recipe suggestions for thyme. They are great substitutes for each other.

Yarrow

If you have a lawn, there's probably some yarrow in it right now. It's native to North America and thrives in many climates.

Yarrow is known for its clusters of red, yellow, or white flowers. Pollinators love it. If you add this herb to your garden, you will be attracting butterflies and hummingbirds. But the flowers are also great in bouquets.

As a food, I like to use yarrow like dill. The foliage is similar, delicate and fern-like. But the flavor has more of an anise bite. It's particularly good on shellfish such as mussels.

How to plant: You can plant yarrow seedlings from cuttings in mid-spring when there's no danger of cold temperatures.

Mature size: More than three feet tall during a single growing season. Give your yarrow plants at least one foot of growing space. Two is better if you keep the plants for more than one year.

Water: Natural rainfall usually is sufficient. If it rains more than once per month where you live, you don't need to water yarrow.

Sun: Full sun

Cuisines: Native American

Maintenance: Yarrow can be invasive. So, pull out plants that have started to encroach on their neighbors.

Warm or Cool: Warm

Flavor: Anise and grassy

Annual or perennial: Perennial

Recipes and uses:

- Steep yarrow in water, alcohol, or dairy to infuse its flavor
- Yarrow tea is classic
- Yarrow cream sauce over spring vegetables
- Clams in yarrow butter
- Yarrow and lavender scones
- Apple pie with yarrow whipped cream
- Other flavors that would pair well with yarrow: chamomile, cucumber, dill, parsnip, fennel, shellfish, lovage, tarragon

Recipes Part III: Desserts

I'm not really a collector. But my cookbook collection is one of my prized possessions. Yes, I use them for recipes. But I like to read the stories too.

I want to understand the reasons why authors cook the way they do. And I especially enjoy reading about how specific recipes came to be.

Two of my favorite books in my collection are The *Alice B. Toklas Cookbook* and *The Taste of Country Cooking* by Edna Lewis. I recommend you pick them up for inspiration. Both connect you to history. Both include exciting ways to use herbs. And both give you a food-based story as interesting as the recipes themselves.

Alice B. Toklas tells you about how she cooked during the German occupation of France in World War II. She had to cook from her garden, with what she could barter, and from the few items on her German ration card.

Edna Lewis tells you stories about growing up in a close-knit community in Virginia during the 60s. There's everything from a "Morning-after-hog-butchering-breakfast" to elaborate Christmas feasts, all cooked from what they had on hand.

But my most inspiring cookbook is my oldest. It's a reprint of a cookbook from 1866. It was written by Malinda Russell and is based on her years of cooking in Tennessee as a free Black woman during the American Civil War. It's a heroic story, and it's a book full of fascinating recipes.

If you love sweets, you'll love this book. Russell ran a cake shop for more than a decade. So, this book has over 70 cake recipes among the other dessert recipes.

Another theme in her cookbook is marjoram. It must have been her favorite herb. She calls it marjorie, and it shows up in a number of recipes in her book. She's the reason I'm a marjoram lover now.

Most people probably think of marjoram as a savory herb. But, after reading Russell's book, I got to experimenting with using marjoram in sweet dishes. The cookie recipe in this section is the result.

The reviews on these cookies were fabulous. They are buttery and almost fluffy. I served them as sandwich cookies with an orange zest buttercream between them.

The rest of the recipes in this section have stories, too. But there's no room to share all of that here. I don't want a 300-page book! And there needs to be room for you to start making your own herb stories. You're the storyteller now.

Mint Granita

The flavors in this dessert are firing on all cylinders. It's sweet and sour and creamy and refreshing. And it's got an herb as the star ingredient.

Ingredients:
6 cups cold water
2 cups sugar
2 cups light corn syrup
6 limes (juiced and zested)
Fresh mint sprigs
5 fresh peaches, diced
3 oz sweetened condensed milk

1. De-stem your mint.

2. Bring the water to a boil and add the mint.

3. When the level of mintiness is acceptable to you, remove the leaves from the water.

4. Dissolve the sugar into the mint tea.

5. Cook until the mixture is syrupy.

6. Allow to cool.

7. Add the lime juice to the cooled mixture.

8. Pour the mixture into freezer trays and freeze.

9. Serve in dessert glasses with peaches, a drizzle of sweetened milk, lime zest, and a sprig of mint as garnish.

Marjoram butter cookies

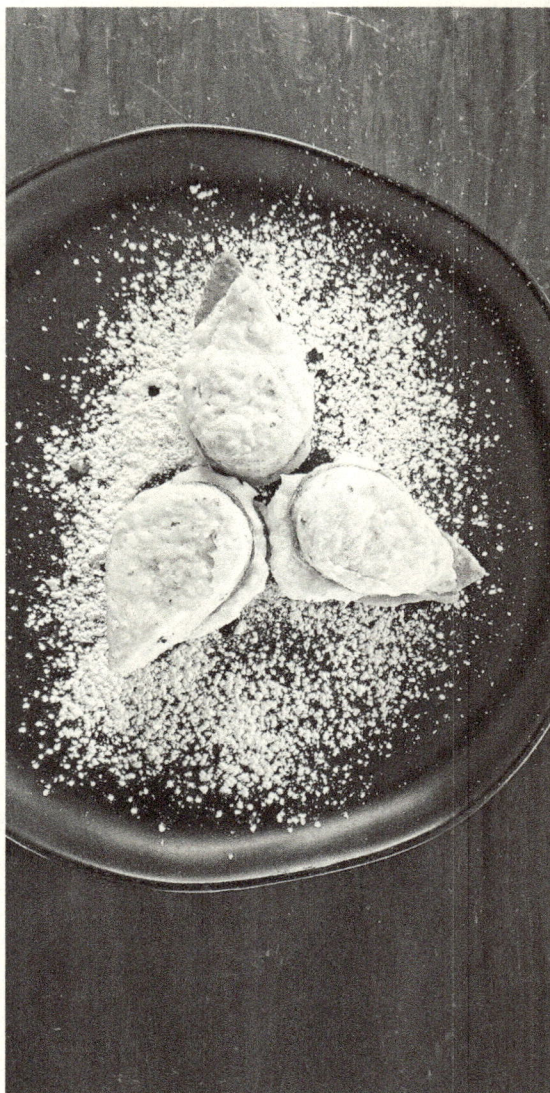

Marjoram has citrus notes, which make it great in a butter cookie. You'll see. Try it. You could also serve these cookies with the mint granita recipe above.

Ingredients:

1 cup sugar

1 cup butter

1 cup sour cream

2.5 cups flour

2 tbsps marjoram, chopped

1. Mix all ingredients together until a dough forms.

2. Chill in the fridge for 30 minutes.

3. Roll out the dough to ¼".

4. Cut into 2" rounds and place on a baking tray lined with parchment.

5. Bake at 350F for 30 minutes.

Candied rose petals

This is a quick, simple, and super elegant recipe. Add these petals to fruit salads and savory salads. Use them as a topper on cakes. You can even add them to charcuterie boards.

Ingredients:
1 cup rose petals
1 egg white
¼ cup granulated sugar

1. Dip the rose petal in the egg white.

2. Coat the rose petal in sugar.

3. Let the rose petals dry for at least four hours before using them.

A weed is a plant that has mastered every survival skill except for learning how to grow in rows.
—*Doug Larson*

Chapter 6:

Designing your herb garden

Look how far you've come. You understand the steps to make an herb garden. You have the tools you need to build it. You have a list of herbs based on your preferences. You also know what each plant needs to thrive. Your next step is to match these plants to your space. You need to decide where they will go. In other words, you need a design. That's what we'll tackle in this chapter.

Designing your garden doesn't have to be a linear process. You can go back and review the herb information in chapter five again or your first plant selection steps in chapter four to revise your list as much as you want.

Also, remember, your herb garden doesn't have to be a contiguous space. You can think of your entire space as your herb garden. There can be plants in any room or any place that you choose. You can live in an herb garden! How wonderful is that?

But how big should your herb garden be? This really depends on how much time, experience, and motivation you have. If you have a lot of time, a low-maintenance design, and lots of experience, go all out and plant as much as you want. If you're just starting, your plan should be much less ambitious. So, depending on your situation, the size of your garden can range from just a few plants to an entire yard or plot. Let's talk about what makes sense.

If you're just starting out

If these are your very first few plants, including decorative plants, start small. My suggestion is just to grow four plants. Pick one plant from each of the categories in Chapter 3.

Get one plant because it's an herb that you love to eat. Get another plant that's used in a cuisine you love. Get a third plant that's a wildcard or rare for you. And get one plant that you think will absolutely thrive in your space.

Also, if you're just starting out, I suggest buying relatively mature plants that are already potted if you can. Seedlings could also work. You don't need to worry about seed starting for now if you don't have to. Go to your farmer's market or home improvement store and pick the healthiest-looking plants you see.

Talk to the staff for suggestions about growing them in your area. Tell them where you plan to put the plants. Then ask how much you should water it given those conditions. Also, ask what other care recommendations they have.

Care for plants in their pots for a month based on the information in this book and what you heard from your local expert. If they are doing well, keep adding one herb from each category to your collection each month. Go back to the store and pick a few more plants. Chat with staff again. And start your care routine again.

I would say you have a fully fledged garden when you get to 12 to 16 plants in about 3 to 4 months. Maybe you'll be happy with what you have. Or maybe you'll decide you want more. It's really your choice. But, with a semester of successful herb gardening under your belt, you're ready to move to herb gardening 102.

This is a good way to start because it's quick and gives you all the joy of herb growing with minimal work and problems. But this process only works well in early spring to early summer in some locations. After that, depending on where you live, you may not be able to find seedlings. In areas with shorter or more defined growing seasons, seedlings only show up when the weather permits growing them outdoors.

If it's out of season when the gardening bug hits you, buy an herb gardening kit. In this case, you'll have to start from seeds. The kits usually do an excellent job of making the seed sprouting process as easy as possible. But, it is a slower process.

When you have successfully grown your new seedlings to six or eight inches tall, you pass. Buy a new kit and keep trying until you have 12 to 16 healthy herb plants. This may take up to 6 months, depending on where you live.

You can also mix and match this process. Start with kits if no seedlings are available. Then, move to seedlings when they become available.

The reason I suggest 12 to 16 plants as a goal is that this is enough to really use in your cooking. You'll be able to experiment with the herbs, substituting fresh for dry or swapping out common herbs for rare ones in your recipes. You'll have enough herbs to practice different knife cuts: chopping, chiffonade, and slicing. You'll have enough variety to use herbs daily in the meals you cook.

A bit of fresh mint in your morning smoothie or on top of your granola and yogurt will make a great start to your day. A leaf or two of fresh basil really wakes up any lunchtime sandwich. Some chopped fresh parsley leaves added to your dinner salad or sprinkled over your bowl of soup changes the game. And once you've changed the game, it's time to change your life.

After you've grown about a dozen plants, you're ready to get gourmet. At this level, you will be able to make memory-making meals.

At this next level, you likely want some pots and beds. You will have plants that require different conditions. You will have plants starting in different parts of the year. You will be growing and eating seasonally. You will be eating fresher and tastier food. And you'll be having more fun. And it only takes six months to get here.

Don't fret if you're just starting out. You'll have a full-fledged herb garden in no time. Here's what you need to think about when you get there.

Common garden designs

There are entire books on garden design. I can't cover everything here. So, I'll cover some easy ones to get you started. Let's think about layout first.

The square-foot garden is growing in popularity. It allows for very dense planting, and its organization lends itself to a beautiful appearance. With this plan, you divide your beds into one-foot by-one-foot sections and plant a different plant in each.

I use square-foot gardening in my own beds. So, I may have nine chives plants in a section. And I may have three of these sections or three-square feet. Meanwhile, there would only be three oregano plants in the same-sized section nearby.

A four-square layout has four beds or four sections, each designated for different types of plants. You can decide which category you will use to organize these beds. You can plant the vigorous plants altogether and move down that continuum. You could also separate by medicinal, aromatic, culinary, and ornamental herbs. Or maybe you separate the herbs by cuisine or other functional use, such as an herb salad bed with all the leafy greens. It's really up to you.

A row garden is what most farms use. It has long rows from north to south. The tallest herbs are planted in the north, with plant height descending as you move south. This orientation helps the plants capture the most sun. And it keeps the taller plants from shading the smaller ones.

Space and access

There are just a few points to consider here. Assume all these ideas apply to beds and pots equally. Basically, you want to make sure there's space for *you* in your garden. And you need to make sure there's space for each plant you want in your garden.

If you have a grouping of plants in pots or beds, start by considering a spine. This will be your main pathway, the space to bring large materials into the garden and take large stuff out. If you can, allow three feet for this pathway.

Stick to pots or beds that are no more than three feet wide. People—including kids—of most sizes will have no problems working in a bed that big. You want pots or beds that you can reach all the way across without too much strain. Four feet would be the absolute max.

If you can, try to get containers that measure as close to a full-foot number as you can. For example, get a two-foot or three-foot container before an 18-inch one. This will make laying out your plants much easier. The math of it will be easier since many references are based on planting density per square foot.

Make sure you have at least one foot on all sides of your pots or beds. A foot and a half is ideal. That way, you can access the plants from all sides. If that's not possible because it's next to a fence, window, or another barrier, put it in a container that can turn. If that's not possible, just put your tallest plants at the back and your smallest at the front. Since your beds won't be very wide, you'll still be able to reach everything.

If you can't reach it, you can't maintain it. If you can't maintain it, it won't thrive. If it doesn't thrive, you won't have much of it to eat. That's why access to your plants is so important. But planning for it doesn't have to be complicated.

To get the maximum yield from each herb plant, you'll need to give it space. Some herb plants require four feet of space. Some require just one foot. Others, you can plant 16 plants to a foot. You'll need to know if you have enough room to grow what you want in a particular area. The information in chapter five gives you the mature size of the plant. You can use this to determine how many plants you can put in each area.

This might seem like a lot to think about. But you really only have to do these steps once. If you find a pot or a bed size that works, buy as many of them as you need to build out your garden rather than making everything unique. That will save you a lot of time and potential overwhelm.

These are the basics to create a layout for your garden. Now that you have them, you can make a simple garden layout with boxes representing each space.

For each box in your garden plan, put the length and width in feet to give you a rough idea of the potential number of plants that can go there.

If you want a more detailed plan based on your hand-drawn layout, get out your tape measure and go for it. I like the garden design software at growveg.com. It has a multitude of features. But at its core is the ability to make a dimensioned drawing of your space. It also helps you with companion planting, succession planting and tells you how many plants you can put in an area. But it doesn't have features that help you with what's coming next.

Beauty

The best gardens are as beautiful and inviting as they are productive. Herb gardens are, by their nature, beautiful. They are green and leafy. They smell great. They also attract birds and pollinators. And with a bit of thought—and not a lot more work—you can have a garden as beautiful as you see in magazines.

At the core of making beautiful things is visual harmony, picking things that match each other. Using the same materials in your garden is the easiest way to do this. Use the same kind of pot or garden bed materials throughout your garden. Use the same mulch everywhere. If there are more than three of something in your garden, make sure they match.

Next, bring in a bit of color. Most gardens are overwhelmingly green, brown, and grey. So, you want your colors to contrast these. Think of the yellow, red, blue, or purple things you can add to create a bit of interest. Maybe one of these is your favorite color. Choose that one. You don't need to add all of these colors. Just two is fine. And spread them throughout your garden in small doses.

You can add colorful flowers and ornaments to get this needed splash of color. Flags and wind chimes are great because they add movement and sound, which keeps away animals that want to eat your herbs. Or you can just paint it on. Add a bit of paint to fences, walls, or doors to add some color too.

Another way to make your garden inviting is to add destinations and an entrance. Think about how nice it would be to sit among your herb plants and read a book, drink a glass of lemonade, or listen to the birds. So, add a place to sit if you have the room.

Your entrance could be a physical barrier, like a trellis, a gate, or a door. But you can also mark an entrance with two fence posts in the ground, a flag, or a sign. The point of the entrance is to give people a sense that they are entering a special place. And they are. This is the source of all the flavor and aromas in the food you feed them.

My last suggestion is to cover as much bare dirt in your garden as possible. In nature, you rarely see the bare ground in areas that feel alive and verdant. Bare dirt or sand feels barren, like things won't grow there.

In nature, leaves, moss, and rocks will cover every empty space. Or, there will be new plants sprouting up to fill the space. Apply this idea to your garden.

You want to plant as densely as possible to make your garden feel lush. And if you have unplanted areas, add coverings like mulch or gravel. You can even use bricks to fill in areas like pathways. If these develop moss between the cracks over time, that's even better. An additional benefit of covering bare ground is that it will keep weeds from sprouting up everywhere. So, it adds beauty and makes your herb garden easier to maintain.

Now, add markers to your design for where you will add color, a place to sit, your entrance, and how you will cover up bare ground.

The sun

Let's focus on the sun for the moment since it's the energy source for your plants. The southern-facing part of your garden would be in the sun all day. Plant warm-season herbs such as basil, sage, oregano, and mint in that part of the garden.

A north-facing garden would be the opposite. You'll need to put veggies here that only want to deal with the sun for half the day or less. Chervil, chives dill, and tarragon would all do well in a place like this. You can also get away with the tallest of your herbs here if they are tall enough to peek over whatever is blocking the sun. Borage and fennel might fall into this category.

Spaces that face east will get the cooler morning sun but will be in the shade the rest of the day. So plant herbs that only want partial sun here. Herbs that you want to have lots of deep green leaves are great here. Cilantro, bee balm, parsley, and lovage would all like it in a space like this. You could also plant leafy greens that you will use as herbs here. That might include arugula, dock, sorrel, or chicory.

Western-facing gardens will get lots of hot evening sun but little sun in the morning. Many of the same plants you planted in the south and east will also tolerate these conditions. But the biggest opportunity here, in my opinion, is for flowers. Nasturtium, calendula, bee balm, and lavender would all be great choices here. You can even grow leafy plants that make lovely flowers here, such as dill, cilantro, and oregano.

So, this is the sun hierarchy. South is the sunniest. North is the shadiest. And east and west are in between. But watch out for sunblocks. This might be your neighbor's house, a large tree, or even a tall fence or shrub. This is important because moving a plant a few feet over could give it enough sun to thrive. Or maybe you'll see opportunities to add partial sun plants on the 'hot' side of the house due to a sunblock, such as a tree or even just a taller plant.

Start with small pots or rollable beds if you're unsure about your design or just want some flexibility. This will give you the option to move your plants around. If you see something dying back from too much sun, you can move it to a shadier spot. If something is getting leggy because it's not getting enough sun, you can move it into a bit sunnier spot. With your design, your feet-on-the-ground surveillance, and the ability to move the plants, you'll have three layers of security to ensure that your plants get the light they need.

These same ideas hold true indoors. Give the sun-loving herbs the sunnier windows and the more delicate herbs the shadier ones.

And since they are in pots, you can move them as needed to find a sweet spot.

You can always add grow lights indoors if you need to augment. Or, put the plants deeper into the house–rather than directly next to the window–to give them more shade.

Now for each area of your garden, mark how much sun it gets: full sun, part sun, or part shade.

The wind

Strong winds pull plants by their roots, break off leaves from stems, and blow away your precious soil. It also has a cooling effect, which may not be good for plants that like it hot. But you want some wind or breezes for pollination and transpiration. This is a plant's version of sweating and helps keep it cool.

If your area is windy, you can do several things to break the wind. You can plant a natural windbreak, build a fence, use windbreak material, or plant in less windy areas. Or just move plants indoors when needed.

The most effective windbreaks reduce wind speed by up to 60%. So, you can reduce 30 mph winds down to 10 mph with a good windbreak. And they can protect an area about 20 times the height of your tallest plant in the windbreak. So if you have a shrub that's three feet tall, you'll get wind protection up to 60 feet into your garden. This assumes a windbreak that's ten times as long as it is high. But, if you don't have that much space, make it as long as it makes sense and looks nice.

Windbreaks should directly face the most common wind direction in your area. You probably have a sense of this if you've lived in your place for a growing season. But if you need to find the prevailing wind direction in your area, check out globalwindatlas.info. After you enter the coordinates of your house, the application will show you a wind rose.

The longest cone is the most common wind direction in your area. You want to put your windbreak directly across this cone at a 90-degree angle.

There may be more than one wind direction in your area. It's up to you whether you install windbreaks for more than one. But be aware that windbreaks will also be sunblocks for nearby plants.

A planted windbreak would be at least two rows of plants at different heights, which together slow the wind down. Ideally, you should plant them spaced at twice their mature size. So, the main trunk of a shrub that's three feet wide would be six feet away from the trunk of its next neighbor. That way, some air can still get through.

A slatted fence or even an engineered fabric panel that touches the ground can also serve as a windbreak. Whatever you use, you want a material that lets some air through. So, a slatted fence is better than a non-porous one.

You can even use your house as a windbreak. That means choosing to put the most delicate plants on the downwind side of your house if they will get enough sun there.

So, for each area of your garden, mark how much wind it gets: calm, light, or strong.

Place the plants

You should now have a blank-slate garden plan with enough information to decide where each plant should go. You know the sizes of the areas where you can plant. You know how much sun each area will get. And, you know if it's windy or not in each section.

Your next step is to make the best match between the conditions in your garden plan and the conditions for each plant in your list. Once you know that, you can decide how many plants should go there. For example, one basil plant might take up one square foot in the south or west-facing garden. You could plant four parsley plants in a square foot of your east-facing garden, where they'll get lovely morning sun.

Within a bed, you can think about planting in the same way. Plant parsley on the east side of a bed or pot and put basil on the west. Put the tallest plants in the center. But, if it's against a wall, put the tallest plants at the back of the bed.

So, for each area of the garden, write the name of each plant you want to go in each area and their number.

And there you have it. All it took was a few pages to walk you through your personalized design. It's personal because it has plants you love. It has the colors you love. And it's designed so that the plants will thrive. And it has spaces designed for you to sit and enjoy it all.

Now, it's time to get your hands dirty. That's right. It's time to plant.

Chapter 7:

Planting and caring for your herb garden

It's time to break a sweat. But trust me, it will be worth it. I think a newly planted garden is one of the prettiest sights on the planet. You will definitely want to take a picture of it and share it with friends and family. Maybe when you have your first meal featuring fresh herbs from the garden, you can show photos of all the baby plants that are now on the table.

This may also be your first time breaking out all the fun new tools you bought for this day. If you're planting in pots, get that hand shovel ready. If you're in plots or bed, you'll need a full-sized shovel and a garden fork or something to break up the soil. You'll also still need that hand shovel. It's versatile.

Prepping pots

For indoor and outdoor pots, make sure you have drainage holes. You can use a drill to make about four in the bottom of the pot if there are none. Next, add a layer of large loose rocks. This creates space for excess water to find its way out.

If your pot is outdoors or on a patio, you can place it directly on the ground. But this might stain your concrete, bricks, or other porous material underneath them. Add a few pot feet to keep the pot a few inches off the ground if staining is a concern. If your pot is entirely indoors, place a tray underneath to catch the water.

Now, you can add potting mix. This will be different from bagged garden soil. It's looser than garden soil so that more air can move around the roots. Wet roots mean rot, which can kill the plant. Potting mix is also sterile to reduce plant diseases. It's also free of other plant material, such as seeds, which could sprout and cause more work weeding.

Some fancier potting mix blends also include fertilizers and other amendments to help plant growth. Because it's a special blend, potting mix is usually more expensive than garden soil. And the blends with more complex ingredients will be even more expensive. It's up to you whether you go fancy or basic in the world of potting mix.

Prepping beds

For folk working in beds outdoors, you want to start by marking out your bed. You likely decided what material you will use for this in chapter three. But it can be as simple as a small trench, posts with rope between them, or a boundary of stones or bricks. Or maybe you use lumber or logs as a border.

You may want raised beds or mounds if you live in a cool area. Beds above ground level warm up faster than those directly in the ground. That extra bit of heat helps the plants grow more quickly.

A sunken bed may be better if you live in a warm area. The dirt in the shallow hole will be cooler than dirt on the surface.

Waffle beds are sunken beds with dirt mounded up all around them. Usually, each square foot is surrounded by mounds. And the mounds are grouped together to form beds. This is more common in the hot and dry southwest. The image you see above is a Zuni garden plan from a Native American tribe of New Mexico and Arizona.

Next, remove any rocks, plants, or grass from the area you want to plant. Once the area is clear, test the soil that is now visible. This is really important for sites that you've never planted in before. You don't know anything about the health of the soil. Most garden centers or home improvement stores will have soil test kits.

Once you know what the soil needs, you can add what's missing. Adding manure, compost, or other organic materials are common options. You might even add a few bags of garden soil to your bed.

The classic method of prepping soil is to turn it with your garden rake to loosen it and mix in your amendments. Once the soil is loose and relatively level, you're ready to plant.

Your first planting

By first planting, I'm referring to your first planting of cool crops during the growing season. Chives, mint, cilantro, dill, parsley, and rosemary all fit this bill. So, there are lots of delicious and fragrant options for this planting.

If you live in a temperate climate, your first planting will probably be in the spring. Wait until the ground has thawed if it freezes where you live. A soil temperature between 65 and 75 degrees is perfect.

Also, wait until the ground has dried from the snowmelt or rain. If the ground is still saturated with water, the soil will make solid clumps. Plants need loose soil so that their roots can grow down into it.

With compacted or wet soil, the roots will grow outwards horizontally. A shallower root system means the plant won't be able to access deeper water and nutrients in the soil. They will run into and compete with their neighbors' roots more quickly. So, your herbs won't be as healthy.

Be prepared to add some frost or cold protection in case of a fluke chilly night. You can add plastic floating row covers over small plants. They are made of material that's light enough to prevent damaging plants. For larger plants, you can use a floating row cover where the plastic is wrapped over semi-circular tubes so that it doesn't touch the plants directly.

Using cold protection in your garden is similar to using curtains in your house. At night, you close the curtains to help keep the heat in. And you open them when the sun comes out and starts to warm things up. The same is true for your row coverings. Take them off when it's above 50 degrees.

You can also make a simple cloche to cover individual plants. Cut the bottom off a two-liter bottle or larger and place it over your plant. Leave the top on overnight to hold in heat. But take it off during the day so the heat can escape.

For some gardeners, there will be a balance between aesthetics and getting a head start on the season. After all, this is the place you live, not a working farm. So, if you're looking for a more stylish–versus DIY–appearance for cold weather, cloches are my suggestion. You can pick up a packet at your local garden center that is reusable, stylish, and affordable for small gardens. If your garden is larger, you may want to use row covers for cost reasons.

Cold frames are more permanent and sturdy versions of a cloche and can also be visually appealing. Usually, they have wooden sides but still use a plastic or glass top. A cold frame might be a good investment if you use the same spot for cold-season herbs year after year.

If you live in a very hot climate, your first planting will probably be in late September or October. This is the beginning of fall when the weather is starting to cool down a bit.

Desert high temperatures might still hit 100 degrees at this time of year. So, plan on planting from seedlings primarily. And give them lots of shade. You can install a shade cover above them or plant them on the side of your land that's shaded from the hot afternoon sun.

The weather is different every year. So, rely on conditions as they are that year. If you're in a temperate area and nighttime temperatures are still dipping below 60 degrees, that's a concern. If you're in the desert and daytime highs are still above 110 degrees, that's also a concern. In both cases, it would be better to wait a bit than risk killing or stunting your plants.

After you've got your first round of plants in, it's time to add your decorations. All the moveable items can be added, like any plant placards with names, flags, or trellises. The only thing left to do now is to memorialize this moment with a few pictures.

Weekly succession planting

After you get your first set of plants in, you can keep adding more seeds to your pots or your beds if you have the space. Herbs have a more delicate flavor when the plant is young. So, the more young plants you have, the more of this delicate freshness you can enjoy.

You can plant some new herbs seeds every two weeks if you want to succession plant. This strategy will work for many of your favorite herbs. You can do this with dill, fennel, cilantro, and parsley. You can also plant new herbaceous greens and lettuces this way.

Arugula, mizuna, and sorrel are great for succession planting. Your new plants will be at their peak in about six weeks. Or you can cut them when they are microgreens, just two or three weeks after you planted them.

This kind of succession planting is perfect for herbs that are prone to bolt too. In this stage, the plant focuses on growing long flower stalks rather than concentrating on leaves. The leaves turn bitter, and the plant slows down on making new leaves. All the plants mentioned in this section bolt. So, they are excellent candidates for succession planting.

Heat is what causes these plants to bolt. So, give these plants some shade in the afternoon when the warm season comes. This is true even for the young ones. If you see a flower stalk starting, cut it off as early as possible to get a bit more life out of that plant.

If you catch a bolted plant too late, you can still use the leaves as flavorings in sautes or to flavor pickles. Any recipe with lots of fats or acid will be good for these more bitter leaves. Or just pull it and plant another.

On the other hand, herb flowers are beautiful and delicious. So, it's your choice whether to let some plants develop flowers to use in your dishes. You may also want to let some plants go to seed so you can eat them or plant them.

Warm season planting

Basil, sage, mint, and stevia all love it hot. These and other warm-season plants want warm soil and warm air temperatures to germinate or to grow. So, plant them when temperatures start to rise in your area. In a temperate place, this might be late spring. In a hot place, this will be around February. You can read about other plants that like warm weather in chapter 5.

There are two choices here about how to plant for the warm season. Maybe you leave areas open at the start of your growing season in preparation for your warm-season planting. Or you can pull things that don't like it warm and put in the things that do. I always think denser planting is better than having sparse areas in your garden. So, I opt for option two if I have the time.

Make sure you remove the old plant completely, including the roots. Put a bit of compost or manure in the hole left by the plant. Then you're ready to add seeds or your seedlings. You could also chop up the old plant and use it as mulching material. Or, add it to your compost pile.

Note that warm weather is not the same as hot weather. Some herbs may struggle in the hot afternoon sun of extremely hot areas. They will produce smaller leaves to prevent them from losing water. Your flowers may start to drop around 90 degrees. If you're looking for seeds, pollen is also damaged in the mid-90s. So if your area is likely to hit those temperatures, consider providing some shade, especially in the afternoons.

During warm weather, plants will need more water. Instead of watering once weekly, you may need to add another day of water unless there's rain. Water early in the morning before the sun gets intense if you can. You don't want the water you just put down to evaporate quickly.

With warm-season plants, you have to be careful when temperatures drop. If you keep the plants in the ground long enough for that to happen, be prepared with cold protection. Because the plants will be mature, you'll likely need a floating row cover or cloches on chilly nights.

A third planting

A third planting of cool-season plants is possible in most places, even in cold places like the upper Great Lakes. This is about August in temperate locations. And you will be able to harvest these plants until it frosts in your area. But, if you don't get frost in your area or use cold protection, you may be able to keep growing through the winter.

Another round of herbaceous lettuces and alliums like chives are perfect to plant at this time of year. These will add zing to great fall salads with other autumnal ingredients such as sweet potatoes, apples, pumpkins, and winter squash.

Or maybe you live in an area with a monsoon season at the end of the summer. This is a great time to plant a monsoon garden. Chervil, celery, and parsley can all thrive in damp conditions.

The ground will be warm when you start your third planting at the end of the hot season. So, these seeds will germinate more quickly than during your cool season planting. That helps them mature fast enough that you can harvest before the cold weather really sets in.

Also, since your third planting will be at the end of the hot weather, your other plants will be large. You can use the shady spots behind your tall hot-weather plants to put in some new cold-weather plants.

But there's another option. If you want to improve the soil in your herb garden, plants cover crops for this third planting. Since you're planting in the fall, you want something that grows quickly, like winter wheat or winter rye. Chop your cover crop down when it matures, but before it goes to seed. Mix it into the soil to give your spring herbs rich soil to grow in.

Maintaining your herb garden

A well-maintained herb garden will need less and less maintenance over time. But, just like every other part of your space, it will need some attention.

You should also plan on making changes as needed. Give yourself at least one growing season to verify that your plan is working. If you notice that something is off, be ready to modify your plan.

Once, I had a vertical garden that was designed for decorative plants. At the last minute, I decided to put herbs in there. It was a disaster. So, I went back to decorative plants, and the garden thrived. It became a jungle, actually!

Things like this vertical garden disaster will happen. Rather than writing off your project as failed, use it as an opportunity to learn more about gardening in general and what works in your space in particular.

The most common and important routine maintenance is watering. Once a week should be sufficient during cooler parts of the season. You may need to increase it to twice a week during the hottest parts of the year. Water as close to the roots as you can. The best way to determine if you've added enough water is to stick your finger into your pot or bed. Your job is done if it's still wet three inches into the soil.

An easy way to tell if you're watering enough is to put some small, shallow containers around your garden. Tuna cans or small measuring cups would do. You can even take small paper cups and cut them down to size. Then water as you normally would. When you're all done, check how much water is in each container. That will give you a good idea of whether you should reduce your watering time or add more.

While you're watering one area, go to the next and remove any dead leaves, debris, and weeds from the next section. All this debris blocks airflow and keeps it wetter inside the plant's canopy. That's a problem since wet conditions promote fungal growth and other diseases. Pull up weeds by the root. Make sure you get all the roots so that it doesn't grow back. Then, cover up that area with mulch.

You want to cut off any damaged parts or dying parts of the plants. Basically, you're pruning your herbs so they can focus on growing more leaves, stems, or whatever part of the plant you're most interested in. The more you prune, the more new growth you will encourage. These young and fresh leaves will be less bitter and give you more of the herbaceous flavor you want from your plants.

Fertilize your herb plants at least every six weeks during the growing season. You won't need to fertilize during the cold or dormant season since growth slows. This is true of outdoor and indoor plants. Use an organic fertilizer since you'll be eating these plants. But it's up to you whether you use granules or a liquid spray.

Even though we love the smell and flavor of herbs, many insects and other pests, such as rodents, don't. For example, the smell of basil, thyme, and garlic are all deterrents. So, you'll likely have fewer problems with pests on herb plants than others. Still, you'll need to keep an eye out.

If you notice aphids or mites, apply an insecticidal soap or oil. Neem oil is a good choice. It's a natural oil from the seed of the Neem tree. You will need to wait a week after the application before eating anything sprayed with Neem oil. Or make sure you wash it really well before eating.

If you notice plant diseases, a liquid copper spray is the answer. It will take care of mildew, blight, slugs, snails, and many other issues. It's organic since it's copper. But you do want to take some precautions while using it. You can mix about two tablespoons in a gallon of water to spray on your plants. That's a solution diluted enough not to hurt you or the plants, but will kill any pathogens.

While applying liquid copper—or any fungicide—make sure you're covered. Wear long sleeves, pants, a mask, and eye protection. Give it 12 hours to dry before you, your kids, or animals hang out in that space. Keep applying it every two weeks until the problem clears.

The best time to spray for slugs and snails is the early morning on a day when it won't rain. You want to spray before the sun is at its full brightness. That's when slugs and snails are still active. And you want to spray on a day when rain won't wash away the spray. This regime will also eliminate any other disease problems you're having.

Recipes Part IV: Herb blends

If you're into life hacks, you'll love using these herb blends. They are an easy way to add flavor to your food with little to no effort. Bring your food to a new level with just a few pinches of each of these blends.

Think of these blends as foundational to your cupboard. If you're new to herbs, keep a few jars of these around to give your kitchen an instant boost into the gourmet realm.

None of these blends include salt. A great way to use these is to whiz them up and add them to salt. That makes seasoning your foods even easier.

Like the rest of the recipes in this book, these blends are ripe for experimentation. Add or replace other herbs you like and with the same flavor profiles to these blends.

On Sundays, I like to prep a bunch of herbs and store them in the fridge for the week. It really only takes a few minutes and makes it impossible not to use these herbs in my cooking.

Now, on to the deliciousness!

Herb de Provence

thyme, basil, rosemary, tarragon, savory, marjoram, oregano,
and bay leaf

These flavors are great with French and Mediterranean cuisine.
Typically, people use a dry blend of these herbs. But think how much
better they will taste when fresh! Mix one chopped tablespoon of
each herb with one crushed bay leaf.

Bouquet Garni

parsley, bay leaves, and thyme

This is another French herb blend. The typical way to use this is to tie the herbs together or put them in a bag. Then, you drop them in your stew, sauce, or soup to add flavor. Because everything's wrapped together, it's easy to remove before serving.

This blend isn't set in stone, though. You can wrap any herbs together you want to add flavor to your dishes.

Herbs fines

parsley, chives, tarragon, and chervil

This is a subtle blend of herbs. So, use it in mild dishes. It's excellent in salads and with fish, poultry, and eggs.

Everything topping

chives, parsley, celery leaf

I keep a container of this blend in my fridge at all times. For me, this is a very American herb blend. I can add these chopped herbs to pretty much anything: baked potatoes, soups, flatbreads, stews, pasta, rice, fish, chicken, and even salads.

If you're the good old American casserole kind of cook–think chili, sloppy joes, baked beans, clam chowder—you'll especially want to keep this blend around.

It's a versatile and super flavorful blend that helps me get more greens into my day. I find that I can get away with up to ½ cup of this blend in a single serving of a dish.

"Herbs are the friend of the physician and the pride of cooks."
~ Charlemagne

Chapter 8:

Cooking and enjoying your herbs

The herbs in your garden are the ones you crave, with the flavors and smells you love. But there's also the aspect that you grew these herbs and cared for them. You watered and tended them. You removed the pests and weeds that stressed them. And hopefully, you spent a few lovely afternoons in your herb garden with a cup of tea.

This bunch of herbs in your hand is your treasure. You must enjoy it, really enjoy it. That's what this chapter is about, getting the most enjoyment out of the herbs you grew. If you don't know how to use them, they won't taste as good as they could and will go to waste. And you don't want to waste your treasure, do you?

Washing your herbs

Even though you will rewash them at home, the herbs you see at the store have likely been through several rounds of washing already. So, don't be surprised if that bunch of herbs you just picked is dirtier than the ones at your local grocer.

It's not hard to wash your own herbs, and the transformation is interesting to behold. Start by washing your herbs off outside. No need to bring all of that dirt into the house. Fill a clean bucket or another container with clean water. Dunk your herbs a few times. Once the water is dirty, pour it out over your garden and repeat. You may need to do this three times.

Your final wash will be in the kitchen sink. Fill your sink with fresh water and dunk your bunch again. You should only need to do this once, but keep it up until the water stays clear after the dunking.

You may not need to do all of these rounds of washing. This is the worst-case scenario. For example, it just rained and splashed mud on the leaves of your plants. Or maybe the wind blew lots of sand and grit onto your plants. Even pulling a nearby plant can throw some dirt onto its neighbors. You need to remove all of that before drying and prepping your herbs.

To dry, shake the herbs a bit to remove some of the water. Next, I use two ways to finish drying my herbs. If I have the time, I spread them out between sheets of paper towel and let them air dry. Once the top layer of the towel gets wet, remove it. You can either put another down or let them air dry.

You can also put your drying herbs in the fridge for a few minutes. The air in there is very dry. But, if you plan to use fresh herbs that day, don't let them stay in the fridge for more than ten minutes, or they'll start to dry out. You also want to place them in the front, since the back of the fridge might start to freeze them.

A salad spinner is another great way to dry your herbs. Just put your bunch in, spin, and Voila. From here, your herbs are ready to store. But let's talk prep first.

Prepping your herbs

Whole-leaf herbs are very decadent to me. They suggest you had enough that you didn't need to chop them up to spread the flavor through your dish. So, let's start there in terms of prepping your herbs.

There are two ways to remove leaves whole from your herbs. For most of your sturdy herbs, you can just run or slide your finger down the stem to remove the leaves. This works for basil, mint, thyme, oregano, tarragon, sage, and other herbs with a stiffer stem.

For more delicate herbs—such as dill, fennel, parsley, lovage, and cilantro—you can pluck each individual leaf or leaflet off by hand. You can also just cut the whole thing up—stem and all—very fine.

Perhaps the easiest way to chop your herbs with larger leaves is to gather them in a pile under your first. Then, start chopping with a large chef's knife. As you chop, move your hand back to expose the unchopped parts. Just make sure you tuck your fingers under so they don't get chopped too. This is a mince.

If your chopped herbs aren't fine enough yet, pass the knife over them a time or two until they are the size you want. The smaller the piece, the more the flavor will spread throughout the dish. It will be more subtle and more blended into the dish. If the pieces are larger, you'll get more dramatic hits of the herb flavor in your food.

You can make strips out of herbs with larger leaves. Just roll them into a cylinder and chop across it. This is called a chiffonade and makes a pretty garnish over drinks or dishes. Basil, mint, and tarragon are great this way.

You'll only want to chiffonade delicate herbs. For example, sage leaves are too thick, and the flavor is too strong to make an appealing result. Shiso has a pleasant flavor, but the leaf is too thick to chew in strips.

Finally, there are alliums. This group of herbs includes chives, green onions, shallots, and garlic. They add a nice and pungent kick and crunch to dishes. But you don't want to mince them. Instead, slice the leaves into tubes across their length. You can cut directly across them, at a 90-degree angle, to the leaf. Or, you can cut at a diagonal for a more elegant look.

Now that your herbs are all prepped, let's get cooking.

Cooking with herbs

One great thing about cooking with herbs is that they can help you eat healthier. You can use them to add a punch of flavor without adding salt, sugar, or fat. They can take any basic dish and elevate it in flavor and style.

But when you're new to using herbs in your food, it can be a bit intimidating. What if something goes wrong? What if your dish doesn't taste good?

I say not to worry about making mistakes. Even if you don't get a step perfect, I can guarantee you that the result with herbs will be much more elevated than without them.

Let's start with the basic ways to use herbs in your cooking.

1. Add them to your spices to make blends, rubs, and marinades.

2. They are great garnishes when just chopped and sprinkled over completed dishes.

3. You can also add them while cooking as a flavoring.

4. You can infuse herbs into liquids such as oil, alcohol, water, vinegar, dairy, and even honey.

5. They are great in chutneys, sauces, gravies, pickles, and dressings.

6. Fry the leaves whole and crunch them up to use as a garnish, or eat them whole as a snack.

7. You can add them to your doughs that you'll bake, fry, or steam.

8. Mix them into your butter, sour cream, mayo, cream cheese, or whipped cream. Have you ever had savory whipped cream? It's delicious.

9. You can candy or sugar them to use for desserts. And this includes many of the herbs you think of as savory only.

10. You can add them to syrups, jams, and marmalades. Again, this includes savory herbs. Get creative.

11. If an herb lends itself to sweet foods, you can chop them finely and add them to pastry cream, frosting, sweetened whipped cream, or ice cream.

An important consideration is whether to use dry or fresh herbs. Although you have a lovely herb garden out back, you probably also have a well-stocked spice rack with tons of dried herbs, too. Both will come in handy, but for different reasons. Use dried for dishes that will cook for a long time. Think pasta sauce, gumbo, or chili. Dried herbs are also great in dry rubs.

Add dried herbs early in your cooking process to give them time to reconstitute and for their flavors to seep into your food. The oils and flavors in dried herbs are more concentrated. They don't have as much water diluting their flavors.

But this is a book about herb gardening. So, let's talk about fresh herbs. You probably have lots of recipes—either in your head or in your cookbook collection—that call for dried herbs. To make a substitution to go from dry to fresh is pretty easy. Use about three times as much as the recipe calls for in dried herbs. So, if your recipe calls for a teaspoon of dried basil, use three teaspoons of fresh, chopped basil.

There are a few other rules to note when using fresh herbs. Their oils are at the most potent since you just picked them. If you add fresh herbs to a cooked dish, do so at the end. You don't want the heat to break the oils down. The more delicate the herb, the less time it should come in contact with heat. For example, your delicate leafy herbs such as parsley, cilantro, dill, and basil can be added right before serving.

This rule about heat applies to herbal teas, too. You will want to steep fresh herbs for about 5 minutes. If you're using an herb that gets bitter, only steep them for three minutes. Herbal flowers fall into this bitter category. Use four tablespoons of freshly chopped herbs per cup of hot water.

Herbs with woodier stems can be cooked into the dish a bit longer. For example, fresh sage, rosemary, bay leaf, or laurel can be added about 15 minutes or more before the end of cooking. Herb stems can also take a bit of heat and will add a lot of flavor to your dish. They are outstanding in stocks. So, don't throw them away. After they've boiled away in your pot, you can add them to your compost pile.

For me, there is also a category of herbs between woody and delicate. These are herbs that can both be cooked a bit and also added right before serving. They are the best of both worlds. And that's why I like to keep these around especially.

Tarragon, marjoram, oregano, and thyme fall into this category and can all be added right before serving or cooked into your dish.

When cooking with edible flowers, focus on the petals. The base and green parts of the plant can be bitter. Flowers can also be treated the same way as the in-between herbs we just discussed. Add them at the end of cooking or chop them up and add them as a garnish to your stew. Imagine a finely chopped mixture of rose petals, thyme, and mint over your lamb stew. You could add the same mix into a salad dressing, steep it into a tea, or infuse the flavors into goat's milk to flavor the base of a dessert mousse.

What dishes are better with fresh herbs?

The real question is what dishes aren't better with fresh herbs. We talked about adding them to salad dressings and directly into salads, sauces, stews, and stocks. We also talked about fresh herb teas. But there's so much more you can do. Before, I offered some generic ideas about using herbs. Below are some actual dishes you can make.

1. Take your favorite fresh herbal tea, add a bit of sugar, and put it in a silicone ice tray. Stick a toothpick into each section when it will stand up. Now, you have popsicles.

2. Mix them into your butter or dough. Imagine hot rosemary biscuits. Or imagine that same chopped rosemary mixed directly into your butter to put on regular biscuits.

3. Make seasoned salts and sugars. A bit of dill ground into sea salt would be delightful over salmon, oysters, or roasted carrots. You can sprinkle a version of this made with sugar over carrot cake cookies, add it to a homemade jar of pickles or rim a cucumber dill martini.

4. Infuse oils, booze, and wine. You could use a bit of lemon balm oil to moisturize dry skin, season a salad, or for dipping your bread. Add fresh basil to your vodka before you make bloody Marys next time. Or add some fresh chamomile, thyme, citrus peel, and sugar to your rosé wine to make a rosé vermouth.

5. Add to dairy. You can steep any of your fresh herbs in dairy to make savory or sweet dishes. Imagine a piece of focaccia with fresh tomatoes, balsamic vinegar, and a basil parmesan mousse with fresh basil from your garden. Or you can just sprinkle a few lemon thyme leaves into your homemade whipped cream to amp up an everyday strawberry shortcake recipe.

For me, using my fresh herbs is just as exciting as growing them. There are so many creative things you can do with them. I've just scratched the surface here. I'm sure you have lots of ideas now, too, because you've read this chapter.

Chapter 9:

Harvesting and storing your herbs

Because you designed your herb garden so well, it is thriving. There is so much abundance that you just can't ignore it. And in fact, harvesting your herbs regularly will help keep the plants healthy.

So, what's the best way to gather all of this abundance? And how do you store all of it? You can only eat so much. What do you do if you've prepped more herbs than you can use? Let's talk about harvesting and storing herbs.

When and how to harvest your herbs

Fruiting vegetables, such as eggplant, squash, or tomatoes, take a while to mature. But you can harvest herb leaves from both your annuals and perennials when the plants are just about four to six inches tall. And many herbs will continue to produce through the fall or until there's a frost. So, your harvests can be seriously prolific.

There's no need to harvest all at once. In fact, I like to only harvest what I will use that day. That way, I will always have the freshest taste possible. But, if you're making a large dish that requires a big chop, never cut more than ⅓ of a single plant. Move to the next plant and the next until you have what you need.

The best time to harvest is in the morning or evening when there's less sun. Just like cooking, the heat of the hot sun starts to break down the flavorful oils in the plant. But sometimes, you need to add lettuce leaf basil, or arugula to your sandwich for lunch, and you'll have to pick your leaves at high noon. It won't kill the plant. But look for a leaf that's getting more shade if you want the most flavorful result.

It's also better to harvest dry leaves. Wet leaves in the morning are soaking up the moisture. They are more delicate during that phase and more prone to damage. So, if there's mud on your leaves from a recent rain or another disturbance, rinse that off. Then, you can wait to harvest until the next day. Or just move to the next section, where there isn't as much dirt.

When cutting your leaves, herbs with long stems can be cut about mid-stem. This includes delicate herbs such as dill, parsley, cilantro, and your woodier ones, including oregano, thyme, sage, and tarragon.

Some herb gardeners like to "pinch" their multi-stem herbs. These are herbs that can develop branches off the main stem, similar to a tree. Basil is most known for this quality. But, it's also true of sage, thyme, tarragon, and several herb flowers such as marigold and geranium.

To pinch, just pluck or cut off the topmost part of the stem between two sets of leaves. You can pinch off just the top set of leaves or pinch more drastically down to about ⅓ off the top of the stem. You can use your fingers to trim delicate herbs in this way. But snips also work.

Personally, I prefer snips because you can tear the plant if you don't pinch it perfectly. Snipping is safer for beginners to prevent damaging your plant.

Pinching and snipping the tops promotes more leaf growth and less flower and seed development. This is important to note because herb flowers and seeds are delicious too. So, you may want to pinch some plants and leave others to develop flowers. It's up to you.

To harvest aliums—plants in the onion family—cut the leaves down to the base. You only need to leave two or three inches for the plant to grow back. Clip a small section from the edge of the plant so that it continues to thrive. You will get about four cuts per year from each section. So, there will be plenty of usable greenery from a single plant.

When flower buds appear, the plant is at a transition. It will slow down leaf production and give that energy to flower production. So, get as many leaves as you can before you see buds. If the buds have opened, it's likely that the leaves on that plant are still edible but a bit more bitter than before.

If you see buds, don't throw them away. All the flowers on your herb plants will be edible and tasty. They are best when they are closed up until they are about half-open. Snip them at the base. You may also want to remove any green parts. These tend to be bitter. The petals are always a good bet. But the delicate flower heads of plants like cilantro and dill can just be gobbled up whole.

If you want to gather some seeds, wait until the flower goes brown and gets dry. This will obviously be at the end of the growing season. On a completely dry day, cut the flower off the stem. Put the dried flowers in a paper bag to continue drying. Once they are completely dry, shake the bag to remove the seeds from the rest of the flower. Your new seeds should be usable for up to three years if you keep them in a cool, dry place.

About one month before the end of your growing season, slow down picking the leaves from your perennials. They will need to make it through the winter or dormant season. You don't want the plant to grow much new foliage that could be damaged in the upcoming extreme weather.

New growth might not harden off to deal with the low temperatures in a temperate climate or the very hot ones in a warm location. So, think about reducing the harvest of your perennials in August in a temperate location or in March in a very hot place.

While you're harvesting, you might as well do some maintenance as well. Snip off any dead or damaged parts of plants. Kill two birds with one stone.

Storing your herbs

If you didn't use up all those herbs you just picked, don't let them go to waste. There are some really easy ways to store them so you can make tasty use of them later.

But before I get into the typical storage methods, I have to say this. Use the ground as your primary method of storage as much as you can. By that, I mean you should be careful not to pick more than you need. Nothing is ever going to be fresher than when freshly picked. Nothing....

If you have some extra chopped herbs left over after the meal, you can freeze them. Put the extra in an ice cube tray and cover them with oil. I suggest you use an oil that's common for you. If you cook more with vegetable oil, use that. If olive oil is your oil of choice, then cover that extra chopped parsley with this oil. But any oil will work. If you're running out of ice cube trays, put the frozen cubes in a plastic bag to make room for more.

Use these oil and herb cubes in a soup, salsa, salad dressing, or stew. Depending on whether the herb is woody or delicate, you can decide when to add that oil cube to the dish.

These cubes are best used in cooked preparations. Thawed herbs won't have the crisp and fresh texture you need in salads or garnish.

Drop the whole cube into your dish if you want an extra bit of unctuousness. Or, you can thaw the cube and use as little or as much of the oil as you want. But it will be hard not to add some oil to the dish you're making.

If you have fresh herbs that are still on their stem, you can pre-treat them. Pretreating is pretty simple. Just cut the stem ends and put the freshly cut ends in a shallow pool of water, similar to the way you'd store cut flowers. You only need an inch of water at the bottom of your dish. Then cover the herbs up with a zip-top bag.

It works even better if you partly seal the bag or use a rubber band to close it off a bit. If you don't have the headspace for standing herbs, put them in a plastic bag with a wet paper towel in it. Wet the paper towel just a bit and close the bag to about 90% so just a small hole remains open. That bag should go into the fridge too.

You should get five days out of your herbs stored in a zip-top bag. But as you go along, you will notice a bit of deterioration. Just remove the rotting or wilting leaves and keep using the rest.

Since this book is about herb gardening, the focus is more on fresh herbs than dry ones. But drying is an important storage method that I couldn't overlook. It's also super easy. You can just tie bunches of herbs with string and hang them up in a dry, well-ventilated place. If you can't hang them up, you can lay them out on a screen in a single layer to dry.

If you live in a humid place, cutting the herbs into smaller pieces will help them dry faster. You can also just remove the leaves from the stem. Make sure that there's space between the pieces so that the air can circulate.

It will take up to ten days for your herbs to dry naturally. To speed up the process, add a fan to the area. Or, you can use a dehydrator or oven to cut the drying time down to just a few hours. Your dehydrator will have specific instructions for that model. So, I won't cover them here.

With your oven, set it at 150 degrees or its lowest setting. You can leave the door open just a bit if your oven won't go low enough.

Perhaps the fastest way to dry herbs is to microwave them. Spread the leaves out on a paper towel. Start out with a cook of 30 seconds on high. Keep zapping them for an additional 30 seconds until they are dry and crispy.

Dried herbs can be used for up to three years. But they won't have as much flavor in the second year. And since you have an herb garden, you can replenish these herbs yearly. So, in my honest opinion, the best reason to dry your herbs is to carry you through the dormant season and before your first harvest of the following year. And what a harvest it will be!

My final request…

Being a smaller author, reviews help me tremendously!

It would mean the world to me if you could leave a review by clicking the image below, which will take you directly to the review section for this book.

Customer reviews

⭐⭐⭐⭐⭐ 5 out of 5

12 customer ratings

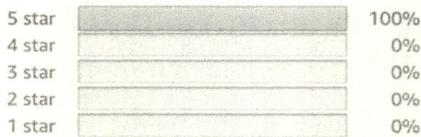

5 star		100%
4 star		0%
3 star		0%
2 star		0%
1 star		0%

ⱽ How does Amazon calculate star ratings?

Review this product

Share your thoughts with other customers

Write a customer review

If you liked reading this book and learned a thing or two, please click this link:

It only takes 30 seconds, but it means so much to me!

Thank you, and I can't wait to see your thoughts.

Recipes Part V: Mains

Herb-forward recipes are tricky. Essentially, you have to make what are usually supporting cast members the star. But you still have all of these charismatic proteins around.

In these recipes, the herbs really shine. And the protein wouldn't be the same without them. They are really a duo. They support each other in the best way. I think of these recipes as being more about the team than about the star player.

Seeded toasted loaded with tuna herb salad

If you have someone in your life that's skeptical of raw fish, try this dish on them. I ambushed a friend of mine with this recipe without telling them the fish was raw. They raved about it. But if raw fish is too far of a stretch for your people, you can use a firm, cooked fish such as cod or salmon.

The creamy butter beans, in contrast to the crispy toast and firm fish, create a textural harmony I enjoy. You can add other items with similar textures if you want more complexity. Creamy avocado, crispy fried shallots would both be delightful additions. You can also sub out the lemon for the acid of your choice. Orange, lime, or an herbed vinegar would all be great here.

One of my favorite herb and fish combinations is dill, shiso, lemon, and salmon. A version of this salad with those ingredients would also be stellar.

Ingredients:
1 lb. cooked butter beans
1 shallot
6 oz. sushi grade tuna, diced
juice of one lemon
1 oz. parsley
1 oz dill
1 oz mint
8 tbsps olive oil
10 slices of toast
salt and pepper to taste

1. Make a vinaigrette from the oil, vinegar, shallots, and herbs.

2. Mix in beans and tuna to the herb salad.

3. Serve on warm toast.

Chicken in tarragon cream sauce

This dish is a classic for a reason. Tarragon and chicken are one of my favorite combinations. It will be tasty no matter how you prepare the chicken: grilled, fried, or baked. But this recipe uses a skillet.

My favorite piece of chicken is the thigh, so that's what I call for here. It doesn't dry out. And it has a lot of tender meat. But most similar recipes for this dish call for breasts. Feel free to substitute pieces if you want.

Ingredients:
1 shallot, diced
2 cloves of garlic, chopped
4 chicken thighs
1 cup of heavy cream
1 tablespoon of butter
2 tbsp tarragon, chopped
2 tbsps white wine
Salt and pepper to taste

1. Heat the shallots in olive oil in your skillet until soft.

2. Add the garlic to the pan and get it soft.

3. Add the chicken thighs and brown them, but don't cook through, about 4 minutes per side.

4. Season chicken with salt and pepper.

5. Add white wine to the skillet and cook for 5 more minutes.

6. Reduce the heat to a simmer and stir in butter, cream, and tarragon to the skillet.

7. Simmer for 7 minutes until the chicken is cooked through and the sauce is warmed.

8. Place thighs on warm plates and spoon the sauce over them.

Basil parmesan pasta

This is a tasty meal you can make any night of the week. Choose any pasta you want. Spaghetti, gnocchi, or fusilli will all be delicious with this dish. Finally, sub out the herbs if you want to try different ones.

To fill out this dish, you can also add any vegetables you want, such as zucchini, peas, or spinach. A bit of bacon or smoked ham would also be tasty here. For a little crunch, add some pine nuts.

Ingredients:
3 tablespoons butter
1 teaspoon garlic
½ cup lemon juice
½ cup white wine
1 tbsp basil fresh, sliced thin
1 tbsp parmesan freshly grated
1 pound pasta
Salt and pepper to taste

1. Boil the pasta in salted water until tender.

2. Simmer garlic and butter together in a saucepan.

3. Add the wine and lemon juice to the butter and simmer for 5 minutes.

4. Stir in the pasta until coated.

5. Turn off the heat and add in the cheese and basil.

6. Serve on warm plates.

Steak bites with mushrooms and herbs

Fried chicken, corn, and cake with something white on it. This is the first menu I ever created. I was six, and my gramma asked me what she should cook for Sunday dinner.

I chose my favorite food and two things I knew you should eat with it. I was learning how to eat.

There's a scene in MFK Fisher's *The Art of Eating* where she had a similar experience. She's in a nice restaurant in Union Station with her foodie uncle.

Before this day, Fisher would just eat "anything" or stick to her favorites at restaurants. For her, choosing her own meal off the menu had been embarrassing and a chore. But following this experience, she could order three harmonious courses after a resolute review of her menu, not including dessert. She really was learning the art of eating, how to eat.

I had a similar experience with my niece, but we were in a chain restaurant, nothing fancy. It was the kind of restaurant you could find in any suburb in any city, anywhere. But even there, I think you can find something interesting to eat.

This evening, I was helping Riviera choose what to eat. And this dish is the dish she chose. That's why I'm including it here, in this book.

If you have anyone in your family that you want to help learn the art of eating herbs, this is a good starter dish. Everyone loves the umami bomb that is beef. But, when you season a dish with herbs like this, you can learn the difference between simply eating to kill hunger and eating to bring joy. I hope that's what Riviera learned that day.

Ingredients:
2 lbs sirloin steak, cubed
1 tbsp olive oil
2 cloves garlic, minced
2 tbsp butter
½ tsp red pepper flakes
1 tsp thyme

1 tsp rosemary, chopped
1 tsp parsley, chopped
1 lb button mushrooms, sliced
Salt and pepper to taste

1. Season the beef cubes all over.

2. Heat oil in a skillet and brown beef when the skillet sizzles. Cook for 2 minutes on each side.

3. Remove the beef from the skillet and soften the garlic.

4. Add the butter and herbs except for parsley and mushrooms, and cook until soft, 8 minutes.

5. Add the beef back into the skillet and warm it through.

6. Turn off the heat and add in the parsley.

7. Serve on a warm plate.

Chapter 10:

It's time to get started!

If you're reading this around planting time, you know what to do and have everything you need to get started on your herb garden.

- You have the list in chapter 2 to help keep you organized and motivated.

- You have your list of herbs that you'll enjoy growing, eating, and using and also that will grow well in your area.

- You have a design that will be easy to maintain and that you'll enjoy hanging out in.

- And you know the tools you need to build it.

- You also know how to harvest, cook, and store them. You even have recipes for inspiration.

Let the fun begin!

I always think it's fun to have a digging party. That's where you have a few people come over to help you with digging or planting or the final prep of the garden. After everything's been dug or planted for the day, serve some pizza and lemonade.

A digging party is a great way to get your friends and family involved and invested in your garden project. That way, when they eat some of your produce, they will feel like they had a part in growing it too. And they did!

When I was a kid, we used to have several of these every spring. For the first party, we'd dig at my grandad's house. Then, we'd dig at ours on another weekend. Then we'd go to the next family member's house. Then, everybody had a garden. It was part of the ritual of the new planting season.

But no matter the time of year, there's always something you can do to enjoy your new hobby. I like to research new seed companies or places to get plants. You can sign up for their catalogs. Most companies usually ship before the start of the growing season. They want you to have time to decide what to buy and have it shipped in time to start your seedlings or plant out.

I suggest you pay special attention to the specific varieties that are available of the herbs you like. There are slight differences that could make one seed or plant better for you than another. You might also find a new variety that seems super interesting to you.

The off-season is also a good time to get in touch with master gardeners in your area. They have loads of information to share and are often underutilized. You could also join some gardening groups in your area. Ask them all of the burning questions you have. They might even be able to review your design with you.

If you're designing your garden during the off-season, take some time to visit thrift stores, flea markets, and farmers' markets. It's a great way to get inspiring ideas about how you want your garden to look. You might even run into a deal on garden tools or garden decor that you must have in your garden.

You should also take a peek at our bonus book and freebies for inspiration. We have a book that lists dozens more herbs you can try out. There's also a book with printables you can use to help you design your garden. It includes sheets you can use as your plant list, a design grid, a seed starting log, and more. The links to access both books are at the beginning of this book.

You could also try your hand with a few herb plants in a pot indoors. There's no wrong time to plant indoors. You can use herbs in your cooking all year round. Greenery always improves the look and feel of space. And in the case of herbs, it can improve the smell too.

If you want to save your energy for your outdoor plantings, you can still experiment with herbs. If they are available at your local grocery store, pick up a few bunches and start experimenting with one of the recipes in this book. The blog Spice and Life also has a ton of great herb-driven recipes to check out.

The herbs you buy at the store won't be as fresh and zingy as your freshly picked ones, but they are a great opportunity to practice using fresh herbs before you have the super prime ones in your hand. And the ones you'll grow will be super-prime!

I'll never forget the first time I grew a basil leaf that was almost as big as my hand. And the first time I made salmon and sorrel from scratch using the plants in the yard was a milestone for me. I also will never forget the salad I made with roasted beets, orange slices, goat cheese, and pickled nasturtium seeds. It was colorful, delicious, and totally inspired by the thriving nasturtium plant I grew.

You'll be able to make memories like this, too, in your herb garden. And I can't wait to read about them.

I get super inspired by garden designs and the tasty dishes you can make from them. You can write to me at greerjacksonbooks@ gmail.com and share what you're up to. I check every message that comes through there.

Let me be the first to wish you much success and lots of good eating from the herbs in your new garden!

Recipes Part VI:
Sauces and toppings

At first, this section was called sauces and garnishes. But I don't really like the word garnishes. It makes it seem like you're adding something extra but not vital.

Topping is somewhat better. But it still suggests something laying on the top, not integral. Nothing could be further from the truth when it comes to herb sauces. Once you start using them, you'll wonder why you didn't know about them earlier. And you'll miss them if they're not there, especially those below.

Just like with herb blends, you can keep these in your fridge to have on hand as you cook through the week. Everything except the crispy sage leaves should last a while in the fridge.

Chimichurri

This is a sauce from Argentina that's excellent on so many meats. Put it on chicken, steak, sausage, and even grilled fish. Serve it at room temperature.

Ingredients:
1 shallot, chopped
3 red jalapeños, chopped
4 garlic cloves, chopped
¼ cup cilantro, chopped
¼ cup parsley, chopped
2 tbsp oregano, chopped
1 cup red wine vinegar
¾ cup olive oil
Salt and pepper to taste

1. Whiz everything together in your food processor.
2. Season to taste. Serve it at room temperature.

Herbed olive oil

This is great with bread, on an egg, and over rice. You can use a blend of herbs or just a single one. It's a great recipe to experiment with too.

6 cloves garlic
1 cup olive oil
4 springs of rosemary

1. Place all ingredients in a clear jam and let set at room temperature for seven days.

Roasted garlic and herb butter sauce

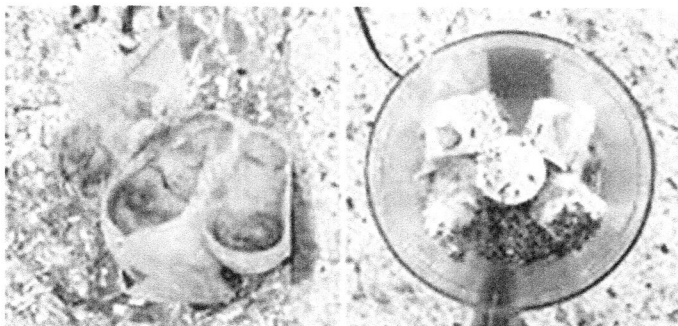

Everything is better with butter, right? Put this sauce on chicken, fish, and even steak.

Ingredients:
1 head garlic, chopped
1 tbsp olive oil
2-½ cups chicken stock
½ half and half
5 tbsp butter
¼ cup parsley, chopped
2 tbsps thyme
1 tbsp oregano, chopped
Salt and pepper to taste

1. Bake the garlic at 350 until browned, about 15 minutes.

2. Combine all the ingredients in a blender.

3. Warm the sauce over a low flame before serving, for 10 minutes.

Lavender-chamomile compound herb butter

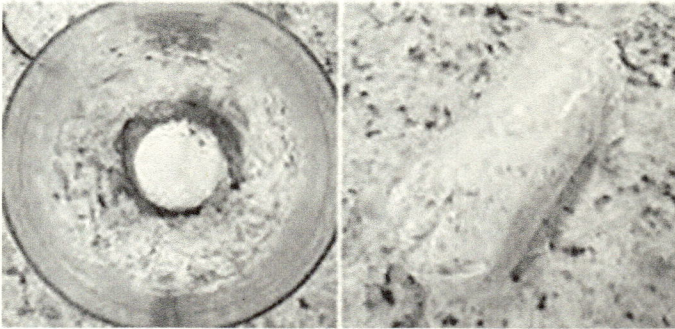

This is a versatile condiment you can store in the fridge until needed. Swap out the herbs I use here with any you like. You can also add spices, sweeteners like jam or honey, cheese, and aromatics, such as hot peppers, garlic, or onions to your compound butter. The basic recipe is ½ cup of butter with up to four tablespoons of herbs.

Ingredients:
½ cup salted butter
1 tbsp thyme, chopped
1 tbsp chamomile petals, chopped
1 tbsp lavender flowers, chopped

1. Let the butter soften so you can stir in the herbs.

2. Combine chopped herbs and flowers into the butter.

3. Spread the butter onto plastic wrap and roll it into a log.

4. Refrigerate the butter until solid.

Infused herbal honey

Use this honey in desserts, on bread, yogurt, or over granola. The basic recipe here is 2 cups of honey to ¼ cups of herbs.

Ingredients:
2 cups honey
⅛ cup bee balm, chopped
⅛ cup lemon verbena, chopped

1. Combine the ingredients in a clear jar.

2. Seal the jar and store it in a warm location for at least a week.

Herbs preserved in oil

This is a great way to store extra chopped herbs. This recipe uses olive oil. But you can also use melted butter.

1. Fill an ice cube tray ¾ full with the herbs of your choice.

2. Cover the herbs with olive oil.

3. Place the ice cube tray in the freezer until the oil freezes.

4. Place the frozen cubes in a plastic bag in your freezer.

Crispy sage leaves

This tasty snack can be crumbled over so many dishes. Use them over salads, soups, stews, and pasta. Or you can just enjoy them as a snack.

Ingredients:
12 sage leaves
½ cup vegetable oil
Salt to taste

1. Heat the oil to 350 degrees.

2. Fry the leaves in batches for one minute.

3. Flip the leaves and fry for two more minutes.

4. Let the leaves drain on paper towel.

5. Immediately salt the leaves while still wet.

Nasturtium seed pickles

Use these as a replacement (or addition) to recipes that include capers. Some people call these nasturtium capers.

Ingredients:
1 cup nasturtium seeds
⅓ cup white vinegar
⅓ cup water
½ teaspoon sugar
2 sprigs of fresh dill
1 tbsp salt

1. Fill a clean jar with washed nasturtium seeds.

2. Bring the remaining ingredients to a boil in a small pot.

3. Pour the hot pickling liquid over the seeds.

4. Seal the jar and store it in a cool place for two weeks.

Pesto

The classic version of pesto is with basil and pine nuts. But there are so many variations. Start by switching out your nuts. Walnuts and pistachios work well. Or switch out the basil for red peppers or arugula. One of the most interesting variations on pesto uses blue basil and lavender. Or you can use cilantro and pumpkin seeds. Parsley and anchovies make a great pesto too.

Ingredients:
2 cups basil leaves
½ cup parmesan cheese, grated
½ cup olive oil
⅓ cup pine nuts
4 cloves garlic
Salt and pepper to taste

1. Combine all the ingredients in a food processor until a chunky sauce forms.

References

Herbs by flavor category

Herbs with the same flavor category make excellent replacements for each other. Mixing herbs in different categories makes for delicious herb blends.

Herb	Category
Agastache	Refreshing
Angelica	Licorice
Arugula	Spicy
Avocado leaf	Licorice
Sweet Basil	Spicy
Blue basil	Spicy
Thai basil	Licorice
Lettuce leaf basil	Spicy
Bay Leaves	Spicy
Bee Balm	Refreshing
Betony	Earthy
Borage	Bitter
Calamint	Refreshing
Carrot Leaves	Sweet
Catmint	Refreshing
Catnip	Refreshing
Celery leaf	Licorice
Chamomile	Sweet

Chervil	Spicy
Chives	Spicy
Cibola	Earthy
Chicory	Bitter
Cilantro	Sour
Dock	Sour
Dill	Licorice
Fennel	Licorice
Lavender	Sweet
Lemon Verbena	Sour
Lemongrass	Sour
Lovage	Licorice
Marjoram	Spicy
Marigold	Sour
Mint	Refreshing
Mizuna	Bitter
Nasturtium	Spicy
Oregano	Spicy
Parsley	Bitter
Peas	Sweet
Purslane	Sour
Radish	Spicy
Roses	Sweet
Rosemary	Pine
Saffron	Sweet

Sage	Pine
Salad Burnet	Sweet
Shiso	Refreshing
Sorrel	Sour
Spring onions	Spicy
Stevia	Sweet
French Tarragon	Licorice
Thyme	Sour
Winter Savory	Pine
Yarrow	Licorice

Herbs by hardiness zone

Herb	Zone
Angelica	4 to 9
Agastache	6 to 10
Arugula	3 to 11
Avocado leaf	10 to 12
Sweet Basil	2 to 11
Blue basil	10 and higher
Thai basil	2 to 11
Lettuce leaf basil	2 to 11
Bay Leaves	8 to 10
Bee Balm	3 to 9
Betony	4 to 8
Borage	3 to 10

Calamint	5 to 7
Carrot Leaves	3 to 10
Catmint	3 to 8
Catnip	3 to 9
Celery leaf	2 to 10
Chamomile	3 to 9
Chervil	3 to 7
Chives	3 to 9
Cibola	4 to 9
Chicory	3 to 10
Cilantro	2 to 11
Dock	4 to 10
Dill	3 to 11
Fennel	4 to 9
Lavender	5 to 9
Lemon Verbena	8 to 11
Lemongrass	10 to 13
Lovage	3 to 9
Marjoram	4 to 10
Marigold	2 to 11
Mint	3 to 8
Mizuna	4 to 9
Nasturtium	2 to 11
Parsley	6 to 9
Peas	2 to 11
Purslane	5 to 10
Radish	2 to 11

Roses	3 to 11
Rosemary	6 to 10
Saffron	5 to 8
Sage	4 to 11
Salad Burnet	4 to 8
Shiso	1 to 11
Sorrel	3 to 10
Spring onions	6 to 9
Stevia	11 and up
French Tarragon	4 to 10
Thyme	5 to 9
Winter Savory	6 to 9
Yarrow	3 to 10

Made in the USA
Las Vegas, NV
09 August 2023